HUMAN SERVICE

HUMAN SERVICE

The Skills AI Can't Replace

JEFF TOISTER

Author's Note

Artificial intelligence only played two roles in writing this book. First, it helpfully suggested the subtitle, "The Skills AI Can't Replace." Second, it helped edit the book's description that appears on the back cover and online listings. All other writing and editing were done by humans.

Acknowledgments

This book is dedicated to the humans of customer service.

You make the experience better.

CONTENTS

Introduction

THIS IS A BOOK ABOUT HUMANS.

You have skills and qualities that are uniquely human. We all do.

These human skills work wonders when serving customers. They can spread joy, decipher complex needs, and overcome obstacles to help your customers have better experiences.

This book will help you identify the natural skills you already have and learn when and how to use them more effectively.

Along the way, I'll draw a distinction between a human and a transactional person. Too many customer service employees check their humanity at the door when they come to work. I call them "automatons" because they act like robots, processing transactions without care or feeling. It's a missed opportunity to help people and find true meaning in customer service work.

We'll also talk about automation, particularly artificial intelligence (AI). It's the elephant in the room, as there are times when it feels like automation is taking over all aspects of customer service. Getting real human help is no longer a given. Instead, it feels like a luxury. Some people worry that automation will completely replace humans in customer service. (It won't.)

AI is speeding up the pace of automation. Call, chat, or email a company, and your first response is likely to come from AI. It also does a lot of work behind the scenes, nudging human employees to say or do the right thing.

This book is not anti-automation. Instead, it's decidedly pro-AI. There are lots of ways AI is enhancing customer service. Some include helping human customer service employees be even more human. I've included a bonus chapter (Chapter Eight) to help you find ways to use AI to unlock your human super-skills.

And there's one huge caveat: AI is a tool. Like any tool, it works best when it's used the right way for the right job. It fails miserably when you try to use it for something it's not capable of doing well. This includes trying to use AI to do a job that requires humanity. You'll see plenty of examples of that throughout the book as well.

What exactly does human service look like? Let's start our adventure with an example.

The shuttle driver

I was bleary-eyed as I boarded the hotel's airport shuttle.

Daylight was just spreading over the horizon. I was joined by a half-dozen other passengers riding the shuttle to the airport. Our driver greeted us as we boarded. His greeting was cheerful, but not too cheerful. It was early.

As he got underway, the driver asked each passenger which airline they were flying. The practical reason for this was so he knew where to drop people off. He also used it to get people talking and to assess the group to see if people actually wanted to talk. Early mornings are a mixed bag of chipper early-birds and half-asleep travel zombies.

A few people in front seemed chatty. The shuttle driver picked up on the cue. "What brought you to our hotel?" he asked. This got them talking more. Other passengers joined the conversation. People had been in town for a mix of business and leisure.

There was a joyful sincerity behind the driver's questions. I could tell he wasn't just making small talk. He was genuinely interested in his passengers, and his questions came from a place of real curiosity. The passengers' answers to the driver's questions allowed him to share suggestions for future visits.

The vibe shifted on the bus. Even the half-awake passengers started showing signs of life. Someone asked a question that got the driver talking about himself. We learned it was a part-time job for him, one he worked a couple of mornings per week. He really enjoyed it.

The short drive felt even shorter thanks to the engaging driver, and we soon arrived at the airport. He stopped at the various airline drop-off points, helped passengers with their luggage, and wished people a fond farewell. People had more energy than they did when they boarded. Their smiles were genuine as they headed into the terminal.

How did the airport shuttle driver take a mundane part of the customer journey and make it memorable? He treated his passengers to human service.

The driver used three uniquely human skills to create a memorable experience.

The first was connection. He greeted customers warmly and sincerely, while still respecting people's boundaries as they boarded the bus.

The second was understanding. The driver asked questions to assess his passengers' basic needs, such as where they needed to be dropped off. He then probed further to feel out which customers would enjoy conversation and used their responses to add extra value—such as making recommendations for future visits.

The third skill was advocacy. The shuttle driver understood that his job was more than just ferrying hotel guests back and forth from the airport. He was the hotel's first impression when he picked up arriving guests, and he was the hotel's last impression when he dropped off departing guests. You could tell the driver genuinely wanted to make each person's experience a little better.

It all seemed effortless. Human service often looks that way. Perhaps it was for this part-time shuttle driver who loved his job. But there's also skill and technique behind the way he served his passengers.

How this book is organized

Most people are naturally equipped with the skills needed to serve humans.

These are the same skills you use to interact with people in other settings. You likely already use human skills to make friends and interact with family members. *Human Service* will help you identify those specific skills and use them more effectively to help customers.

The book begins with a preview of the human advantage in Chapter One. You'll see how an employee saved the day when her coworkers were acting like robots. I'll profile a company that's vaulted ahead of the competition by combining human service with smart automation. And you'll read about one company's experiment that showed how expert humans doubled sales conversions compared to AI.

From there, the book is divided into three sections, each highlighting a specific human skill:

1. Connection

2. Understanding

3. Advocacy

Finally, I've included a bonus chapter on the human-AI partnership. Human service and AI aren't binary choices. There are many ways that humans and AI can work together to deliver consistently great customer experiences.

Who is this book for?

There are two groups of humans I had in mind while writing this book.

The first are employees who serve customers. If that's you, then *Human Service* can help you bring your best human self to work and help customers have consistently great experiences.

The second group of humans are customer service leaders. If you're in that second group, this book will show you how to unlock your team's full potential. It will also offer guidance on when and where human service can give you a competitive advantage.

I'm your human

One theme you'll see throughout this book is that automation is often the first point of contact, but a human needs to be available when customers need or prefer human help.

I'd like to demonstrate that to you. I've created a downloadable workbook companion for this book. You can get a copy of the workbook by using a simple automated process:

1. Go to **humanservicebook.com/workbook**
2. Enter your first name and email address
3. Check your email for the workbook

That automation functions 24/7, but you can easily reach me directly if you have a specific question or would like some extra assistance. There are two options for this.

One option is to reply to the email I use to send your workbook. Your response will go straight to me. No bots or assistants get in the way. I answer my own email and do my best to reply within one business day.

The other option is to contact me directly. Here is my personal phone number and email address:

- Call/text: **619-955-7946**
- Email: **jeff@toistersolutions.com**

Is it a risk to share my personal contact information so freely? No, not really.

I've put my personal contact information in all the books I've published. Doing this has taught me that relatively few readers will contact me directly. Those who do generally have an interesting question, are facing a specific challenge, or have a success story to share. I genuinely enjoy getting these messages and corresponding with people who take concepts I've written about and put them into action.

Getting started

Human readers have different needs, so *Human Service* is intended to be flexible.

You can read the book however you'd like. One way is to go cover to cover, like a traditional book. Or you can choose to skim and scan, looking for the ideas that will help you the most. I've added a recap section at the end of each chapter to make that easier to do.

So, if you're ready, let's get started!

START HERE:

The Human Advantage

CHAPTER ONE

Adding Human Value

TO BE CLEAR, LOSING THE JACKET was my fault. But what happened next was the customer service equivalent of a poke in the eye.

I left the jacket in a rental car in Newark, New Jersey. It was a warm spring day, and I carelessly tossed the jacket into the back seat when I stopped to meet a friend for lunch. It was soon forgotten as I drove from lunch to the airport, dropped off the rental car, and schlepped my way into the terminal. I didn't realize it was missing until I got home to San Diego.

I naively imagined I could contact the rental car company, tell someone where I'd left the jacket, and a helpful employee would retrieve it and ship it home to me.

That's not what happened.

I had to fill out a form on the rental car company's website to start the lost item process. The website explained that someone would contact me once the item was found. In the meantime, I could scour the list of found items to see if my jacket appeared.

The first red flag was that there were no lost items on the list. The rental car facility at Newark is huge. It was hard to believe I was the only distracted traveler who'd lost anything. I began getting nervous about the fate of my jacket.

The second warning sign was a lack of communication. Several days went by with none of the promised updates. I checked the lost-and-found list again and confirmed that Newark had maintained its spotless record of zero reported lost items.

Something felt wrong. I called the rental car company, navigated its maze of phone menus, and was connected to a person. Not a human. A transactional person who acted like an automaton. Someone who clearly didn't care whether or not I was reunited with my jacket.

I tried to explain that the lost-and-found system didn't appear to be working. The transactional person didn't care. All they would tell me was the jacket hadn't been found and I should keep waiting.

Undaunted, I found a direct line to the rental company's Newark location. Surely someone there could go retrieve my jacket. Right?

The rental car company foiled my attempt to get help by re-routing my call to the same contact center as before. Another automaton-person glibly told me the jacket hadn't been found and to allow more time. They weren't interested in hearing my thoughts on the process or my growing concern that the system was broken.

A few more days passed. No updates. Newark was still posting a zero on the lost items scoreboard. Does somebody get a bonus for this?

I decided to escalate and sent a direct message via social media. The message explained my concern that the system was broken and requested help getting my jacket back.

The company's brigade of transactional humans evidently worked for their social media team as well. I messaged with three different people and none were helpful. Here's one of the messages I received:

> *Hello.*
> *I am sorry that you have not heard from our location at Newark yet. I am showing that the status is still pending. Please allow more time to find the items and contact you with how to recover them.*
> *Thanks*
> *Blake*

I'm guessing Blake is a real person, but this message contains no human qualities. Blake was an automaton—a human acting like a robot. There's nothing in the message that solves my problem or makes my experience better. They simply regurgitated what the system showed without acknowledging my concern that the system was likely broken. This message could easily have been automated.

The lack of human service made a simple issue feel miserable. The automated lost-and-found system was clearly broken. The five transactional customer service reps I'd interacted with (two on the phone and three via social media) might as well have been bots. None of them added any human value to the experience by acknowledging that the system was broken, or helping me track down my lost jacket.

Weeks went by. I didn't hear from the rental company and assumed my jacket was lost. I bought a new one. I tried to put the whole lost jacket fiasco behind me.

Then, nearly a month later, the rental car company sent me an email.

> **Subject**: *Lost item update*
> *Dear Jeff,*
> *Unfortunately, your Lost Coat/Jacket has not been located at this time. We will continue to search for your lost item.*
> *Sincerely,*
> *Customer Care*

This email felt like a poke in the eye. Why wait a month to send the promised follow-up? Why write to tell me what I already knew—that my jacket hadn't been found? Why lie and tell me you'd continue to search for my jacket when I had told you exactly where to find it? Why send an update when it was obvious nobody had searched for it in the first place?

They say that an upset customer might tell ten friends about their experience. That number goes up substantially if that upset customer is an author who is looking for an idea for their next book. Time to start researching the madness behind this broken system.

I learned that the rental car company's lost-and-found system was run by a third party. The third party used artificial intelligence (AI) to match lost-and-found inventory with customers. It automated many aspects of the process, including customer notifications. Somehow, that AI decided to message me a month after I filed my claim.

That was just the first email. Nine days later, the AI sent me an identical message. Another followed eight days later. It kept emailing. I received five of these emails over the course of a month. Each one contained exactly the same message. My jacket never appeared. The whole thing felt inhumane.

The experience reminded me of all the other issues I had with this rental car company. Fifty percent of the time, they didn't have the car I reserved. I had to go to the rental car counter 25 percent of the time, despite my frequent-renter status supposedly allowing me to bypass the line and go straight to my car. Then there was the time in Austin when I refused three vehicles with cracked windshields and one vehicle with a flat tire before I was finally given a car that was drivable.

The countless mistakes and frustrating experiences were compounded by uncaring, transactional employees. Nobody ever seemed to make an effort. It was time to make a change.

The scourge of automatons

Companies hire three types of customer service reps: automation, automaton, and human.

Automated customer service reps are machines and software. Automation works wonders—when it works. Customers can effortlessly use automation to make purchases, manage their accounts, and solve simple issues. Companies use it to drive down costs, improve efficiency, and make the customer experience a smoother ride.

AI can make automation better, but it has problems that drive customers bonkers. Many AI bots struggle to understand basic questions like, "When do you open?" or "How do I contact customer service?" AI routinely hallucinates and makes up answers, then stubbornly refuses to escalate issues to a capable human. Sometimes it actively causes harm, like repeatedly sending a customer emails to remind them that they lost their jacket in Newark and nobody's looking for it.

A study by Verizon found that customers' major gripe with AI was being forced to use it, with 47 percent of respondents saying their biggest frustration was the inability to get help from a human.[1]

The second type of customer service rep is the automaton.

Automatons are transactional employees who act more like automated robots than humans. They greet you mechanically, if at all. They don't listen to you or understand your needs. The worst part is that automatons don't care whether or not you have a good experience.

Blake at the rental car company was Exhibit A. There was no warmth in Blake's message. Blake completely missed that my real concern was that the lost-and-found system wasn't working and I was starting to lose hope that I'd get my jacket back. And it was crystal clear that Blake didn't care one bit whether or not my jacket was returned.

Think about your own experiences as a customer. The customer service agent who sounds like a robot when they answer the phone. Cashiers who reflexively ask, "Did you find everything all right?" yet never care about the answer. Retail employees who make themselves scarce by deliberately avoiding customers. All the people who are quick to say "No" or "I can't" when you ask for the most basic level of assistance. None of these automatons make your experience better.

Automatons are worse than automation because at some level, customers expect automation to occasionally fail. But people have a choice. They can try to be helpful, or they can give up and act like robots.

The human is the third type of customer service rep. Humans are so rare that you stop and notice them. Like Ramona, who was the human I needed to get me a refund for a $12 overcharge caused by wonky automation—a problem that automated customer service and three automatons couldn't find a way to solve.

Ramona navigated through a maze of broken systems and corporate hierarchy to get my $12 back. While Ramona's automaton coworkers quickly dismissed my issue and refused to help, she acted like the big sister who stops the school bully from stealing your lunch money.

It would be great if companies could fix their broken systems. It's draining and demoralizing to work for a company where nothing seems to work. I've written an entire book called *Getting Service Right* that describes those problems and the impact they have on employees. Until that day arrives, I want humans like Ramona in my corner.

Characteristics of human service

Human service is more than just a living, breathing person serving a customer.

Human service is genuine. You can tell the person truly cares about your experience and wants to help make it better. These are people like Ramona who are instantly likable, take time to understand your needs, and fiercely advocate on your behalf. Here's the definition I like best:

Human service is using uniquely human qualities to serve others.

These qualities include connection, understanding, and advocacy:

- **Connection:** getting customers to know, like, and trust you.
- **Understanding:** discovering customer intent and empathizing with their emotions.
- **Advocacy:** acting on behalf of the customer to help them have a better experience.

We'll take a closer look at each of these three characteristics throughout this book. You'll explore examples of each one, discover specific techniques you can use to apply these qualities when serving others, and identify the business impact of being human in the right moments.

Human service profile: National Car Rental

My lost jacket experience made me determined to find a more humane car rental company.

A search of leading car rental companies revealed one that was highly rated for frequent travelers like me: National Car Rental. National ranked first in both the American Customer Satisfaction Index[2] and the J.D. Power North America Rental Car Satisfaction Study when I did my research.[3]

My experience with National was like night and day compared to the old company. National blends useful automation with human service to make renting a car an easy—and even enjoyable—experience.

It was easy to use the automated process to create a new customer account on National's website and reserve a car. The smartphone app was intuitive and made it a snap to retrieve my reservation while I was on the go. I felt pretty good as I walked into National's rental car garage in Nashville, Tennessee, to pick up my first rental. Ironically, this was on the same day that I received one of those cold-hearted emails from the old rental car company's AI system.

A friendly National employee greeted me as I entered the garage. It was a genuinely warm greeting—the kind that instantly disarms you and makes you like the other person.

She must have spotted that "am I doing this right?" look on my face, because she offered assistance. I explained it was my first time renting from National and I wanted to make sure I picked out the right car. She patiently explained the process and gave me a few tips for using the app to make renting a vehicle as smooth as possible.

This was what a car rental experience should be! Automation did most of the work to create a seamless rental process. A helpful human (not an automaton!) was available right at the moment of need to add extra value by inspiring confidence and ensuring everything went smoothly.

The National Car Rental employee I encountered at the Nashville airport embodied those three characteristics of human customer service:

1. **Connection:** she built rapport with a warm greeting and by offering assistance.

2. **Understanding:** she listened to clearly understand my needs.

3. **Advocacy:** her actions made it obvious she wanted me to have a good experience.

That was the day that National became my new rental car company. My experiences with it since then have been consistently good. The majority of my interactions are through seamless automation. This includes renting a car, generating the rental agreement, sending automated pick-up and drop-off reminders, and closing out my rental when the car is returned.

It's the friendly humans who make the National experience superior. A helpful National employee in Portland made it easy to change the dates on my rental when I wanted to pick up my car a day early. A kind employee in Boston upgraded me when he greeted me in the garage and learned I just needed a car for the day. A caring employee in Sonoma gave me a comfortable car with good gas mileage when I shared that I would be doing a lot of driving.

The emphasis on human customer service at National Car Rental is no accident. It's clearly outlined in the company's five-point Standard of Care service standards.[4]

1. Complete clean pledge

2. Low-touch transactions

3. **Exceptional customer service**

4. Vehicle maintenance and safety

5. Visual inspection of every vehicle

National defines its exceptional customer service standard this way:

"Great customer service starts with listening. We take the time to understand your needs, so we can offer the best solution. This attention to our customers is what has made us a global leader in mobility. Customers come to us—and stay with us—because we always strive to deliver an exceptional and personalized experience."

As National Car Rental proves, you don't need human service for every step of the customer journey. It's fine to automate those routine, transactional parts where humans aren't needed to add human value. You just need humans in the right places at the right time.

Human service profile: Headset Advisor

Headset Advisor sells phone headsets to businesses whose employees spend a lot of time on the phone. The company's competitive advantage is giving great advice to help customers confidently make the right choice.

Buying a new headset can be a daunting task. There are many models to choose from, and it's hard to know which features and options are right for you. Compatibility is also a concern, since headsets must often work with multiple devices, such as a phone and a computer. Headset Advisor has some helpful tools and product descriptions on its website, but some customers need a little more advice. Those customers can ask questions via chat.

Drew Merritt, a vice president at Headset Advisor, ran an experiment in March 2025. He began using an AI-powered chatbot to answer pre-purchase questions from customers who needed extra help making a purchase.

He quickly noticed customers were really unhappy with it. Customers gave the chatbot a miserable 18 percent satisfaction rating. The results convinced Merritt to switch to using only humans to chat with customers who had questions before making a purchase.

The change made an instant impact. Customer satisfaction soared to 92 percent. Even better, sales conversions doubled! The company's average order value is roughly $300, so the human touch added more than enough revenue to pay for staffing the chat line with humans.

A helpful human in the right place at the right time makes business sense. Humans increased sales at Headset Advisor. National Car Rental leans on human service in the right places to earn customer loyalty and lead the industry in customer satisfaction. Humans like Ramona who helped me get that $12 refund save customers like me from an endless pit of despair when automation breaks down.

Throughout this book, I'll share more examples of industry-leading companies that use human service in the right places. You'll see how companies like Chick-fil-A and Trader Joe's lean into humanity while their lagging competition doubles down on automation. I'll describe examples of human service boosting revenue, improving efficiency, and helping companies build trusted brands. You'll also see how broken automation and transactional humans can cost your business dearly.

Knowing when human service is needed is just the start. You also need to know *how* to use your uniquely human skills to help customers in need. Each of the following chapters is organized by a specific human service skill. It includes examples and techniques you can try to give your customers an even better experience.

In this chapter, we'll start with a technique the first rental car company could have used to find my lost jacket. It's called iceberg hunting.

Exercise: Iceberg hunting

Blake's inhumane response to my plea to help find my jacket made me question my long-standing relationship with that car rental company. The AI-generated emails that taunted me about the jacket pushed me to cancel seven reservations and take my business to a competitor. A lack of humanity cost it thousands of dollars in lost revenue per year from just one customer.

There are lost-jacket moments in every company: situations where a process breaks down, a product doesn't work, or a customer simply needs help and doesn't get it. All it takes is one human to spot the issue and be willing to take charge of solving it.

Iceberg hunting can help you find the lost-jacket moments in your company.

A customer service iceberg is an issue that seems small on the surface, but is really a much bigger issue. Icebergs can be hard to identify at first. You might only receive a complaint or two. In other cases, the problem seems easy to fix but recurs without you noticing.

My lost jacket should have signaled an iceberg. Recall that part of my complaint was that the system didn't appear to be working. There were no promised updates and there were no lost items listed for the rental car facility in Newark. Both of these should have signaled a potential iceberg to any of the five employees who received my complaint.

Icebergs can sometimes hide huge problems. One customer experience leader discovered confusing instructions were causing over $1 million worth of products to be returned every year just because customers couldn't figure out how to use them!

Three steps can help you identify and fix icebergs before they get too big. The first step is to avoid assumptions. Stay vigilant for unusual or unexplained issues. Look out for problems that theoretically can't happen, but somehow happen anyway.

Drew Merritt at Headset Advisor found an iceberg in the middle of our conversation about his AI-bot experiment. Merritt noticed that pre-sale chats had seemed slow lately. He ran the numbers while we were talking and learned pre-sale chats had cratered from 1,200 offers per month to just 150. Fixing the issue added a lot of potential revenue.

The second step is to investigate the issue and dig for the root cause of the problem. You can start by asking, "Why is this happening?" You might need to involve other departments or teams to get an answer.

I once managed a customer service team for a retail catalog. One day, I noticed a lot of backorders for an item we should have had in stock. I went to the warehouse to investigate and discovered a box of the items tucked in a corner. The box was physically there but hadn't been received into inventory. The box contained 25 items that could be used to immediately fill orders at a $100 average order value. That 15-minute investigation generated $2,500 in revenue and made 25 customers happy.

The third step is to solve the problem. Look beyond the individual customer and try to solve the systemic issue.

For example, a customer service leader discovered an iceberg when a customer called to complain about a billing error. The specific error theoretically couldn't happen, but somehow it had. The leader investigated the issue and discovered a problem with the company's billing software that caused a rare but costly mistake affecting several other customers. It took less than an hour for someone in the accounts receivable department to fix the software so the error wouldn't happen again. Resolving that iceberg saved the company $50,000 per year.

Try to find an iceberg in your company that negatively affects your customers' experience:

1. **Avoid assumptions:** look for strange or unusual issues.

2. **Investigate:** find the root cause.

3. **Solve:** fix the underlying problem so the issue won't keep happening.

Let's recap

Humans can add extra value to customer service by using uniquely human qualities. These qualities include connection, understanding, and advocacy.

- **Connection:** getting customers to know, like, and trust you.

- **Understanding:** discovering customer intent and empathizing with their emotions.

- **Advocacy:** acting on behalf of the customer to help them have a better experience.

Try the iceberg-hunting exercise to find opportunities to prevent "lost-jacket" situations by adding human value to difficult or unexpected issues.

In the next chapter, we'll focus on a deceptively simple but important skill: greeting customers.

CHAPTER 1 ENDNOTES

1   FT Longitude, *AI for better CX: How brands can crack the code*, (Verizon, November, 2025).

2   "Satisfaction Benchmarks by Brand, Car Rentals," American Customer Satisfaction Index website, accessed May 20, 2024, https://theacsi.org/industries/travel/car-rentals.

3   "Rental Car Customer Loyalty Hinges on Trust, J.D. Power Finds," J.D. Power, press release, October 9, 2024, https://www.jdpower.com/business/press-releases/2024-north-america-rental-car-satisfaction-study.

4   "Our Standard of Care," National Car Rental website, accessed January 11, 2025, https://www.nationalcar.com/en/support/our-standard-of-care.html.

SECTION ONE:

Connection

CHAPTER TWO

Greetings

A CREDIT UNION CLIENT ASKED ME to talk about greeting customers when I delivered a keynote at their annual employee town hall meeting. They were about to launch a major update to their online banking system. The CEO was counting on friendly, helpful employees to guide credit union members through any bumps in the rollout.

Helping people confidently use technology requires trust. Gaining a member's trust in a branch office or over the phone starts with a warm, welcoming greeting.

I like to use real stories in my presentations to bring concepts to life. Two greetings immediately came to mind as I searched for examples of what an authentic greeting should look like. Neither fit the mold of a typical customer service greeting. Both stood out because they were so human.

The first happened at the now-defunct Westin Portland. I should clarify that the hotel's demise had nothing to do with service quality, which was always excellent. The building's owner decided a number of years ago to leave the Marriott system (the company that owns the Westin brand) and rebrand the hotel.

Years ago, I started a consulting project that required me to travel to Portland, Oregon, every week for several months. I chose the Westin Portland as my home away from home. Ali was the doorperson who greeted me when I arrived to check in the first week of the project.

Ali saw me approaching the door, smiled, made eye contact, and opened the door, saying, "Welcome to the Westin." It was a standard greeting I'd received at countless hotels, but there was something in Ali's delivery that made it feel genuinely welcoming.

He greeted me again as I arrived at the hotel the following week, recognizing me as he opened the door. "Hi, Jeff! Welcome back!" It made me feel extra welcome to be remembered and greeted by name.

The following week was even better. Ali and I had chatted a few times during my previous visits. He beamed as he saw me dragging my suitcase along the sidewalk. "Hi, Jeff!" he said. "Welcome home!"

That wonderfully personalized greeting made me truly feel welcome. Ali conveyed a lot of meaning in just a few words. He remembered my name, knew I was often staying at his hotel, and understood that connection elevated the experience for a guest who was spending a lot of time away from home. It took skill to go beyond the standard script and personalize his greeting. It also showed that Ali honestly cared about his guests and wanted to be there for them.

The second memorable greeting came from Matt at my local True-Value hardware store. Matt saw me walking in and immediately said, "What are YOU doing here?!"

Though the greeting was perfect to me, it probably sounded terrible to any bystander who didn't know the context behind why Matt greeted me like Jerry Seinfeld greeting his arch-nemesis Newman on the show Seinfeld. Hopefully, a mystery shopper wasn't watching, because Matt might have gotten a failing score for delivering such a masterful customer greeting.

Let's rewind just a bit. This was my second visit to the store that day. Matt had helped me on the first visit when I came to get supplies for a home project. He'd spent a lot of time walking around the store to help me get everything I needed.

I joked with Matt that I have bad luck with home projects, and said he'd likely see me later that day because I either forgot to get something on the first visit, or an unexpected problem came up. Matt laughed about it with me, but then assured me that if I did need to come back he would be there to help.

His pitch-perfect greeting on my second visit acknowledged that my project had obviously hit an unexpected snag and my fears were realized—I had to go back to the hardware store. "What are YOU doing here?!" was a fun way to recognize that.

Human greetings like Ali's and Matt's make a huge difference. They're part of the reason why I booked so many nights at the Westin Portland and why I consistently passed by the big box hardware stores to visit my neighborhood TrueValue.

A good greeting seems so simple, yet it's rare. Think about your recent experiences as a customer visiting a store, dining at a restaurant, or calling customer service. Most greetings are robotic and transactional—if you're greeted at all. The human element is missing.

In this chapter, we'll explore the impact of a poor greeting, why companies are tempted to automate the first point of contact, why greetings actually matter, and what makes a good greeting good.

The cost of poor greetings

"Next!" The cashier's greeting at the fast food restaurant was jarring. It set a negative vibe for the entire interaction.

She said just three lines to every customer. "Next!" when it was the next customer's turn. Then an impatient "What'll you have?" when the customer approached the counter, capped off with an exasperated "And your sides?" after the customer ordered their main entree. All were delivered with the tone and inflection of an angry robot.

The cashier didn't say hello, please, or thank you. She never confirmed an order or asked any clarifying questions. She pointed at the order total at the register, as if numbers were banned from her vocabulary. Smiling clearly wasn't on the menu.

This restaurant was in an airport. I was traveling through on a connecting flight and wanted a quick dinner. There were other choices, and the cashier's surly demeanor made me briefly consider them, but I decided to stick it out and watch how other customers reacted.

The line was at least eight people deep, but it could have been longer. Quite a few customers decided to leave after the cashier's unwelcoming demeanor made the restaurant less appetizing. Potential customers saw the line, heard the cashier shout "Next!", and moved on. The restaurant was losing roughly $150 per hour in revenue because the cashier was so unwelcoming.

It was finally my turn. "Next!" shouted the cashier. I approached the counter with a smile and said, "Hi!" The cashier avoided eye contact and stuck to her script. "What'll you have?"

The cashier was an automaton. She didn't add any human value to her work. It was easy to see how actual automation might have improved the experience of placing an order!

Another fast food restaurant was a short walk away. That restaurant seemed to be doing a brisk business even though it had no lines at all. It also had no cashiers. Customers placed their order at an automated kiosk.

Why companies are tempted to automate cashiers

Customer service leaders have privately told me they struggle to hire and train employees to deliver even a basic level of friendly service. Too many are transactional employees like the "Next!" cashier.

Automation solves this problem and appears cheaper over the long run. Grocery and retail stores have expanded self-checkout to save on labor costs and serve customers faster. Subway systems have replaced ticketing agents with automated fare-payment technology. Hotels and airlines drive would-be customers to automated channels like AI-powered chatbots or automated phone menus designed to deflect customer contacts away from costly human reservation agents.

Automation has taken over the first point of contact at many fast food chains. You can use a smartphone app to place orders for pick-up or delivery while earning loyalty points for your purchase. Pull in to the drive-thru lane, and there's a good chance an AI agent will be taking your order. Walk into the dining room, and you'll be prompted to place your order at a kiosk. The unsmiling employees assembling your meal seem to know automation will soon phase out their jobs, too.

Automation gives these businesses a number of advantages. The smartphone app and loyalty program give companies a lot of data on consumer spending habits. Customers are encouraged to pre-load the app with gift cards or cash to make payment easier, which is effectively a no-interest loan to the company. At the end of its 2024 fiscal year, Starbucks was holding a whopping $1.78 billion in cash from customers' unspent gift card balances.[1]

Chains like Taco Bell, Wendy's, and McDonald's are using AI to take drive-thru orders and reporting positive results after some initial challenges.[2] AI promises to be faster, more accurate, and easier for customers to understand. It also frees up busy employees inside the restaurant to concentrate on other tasks.[3]

Order kiosks in restaurant dining rooms are rapidly replacing cashiers. Yum Brands—the parent company of Taco Bell, KFC, and Pizza Hut—found that replacing cashiers with kiosks increased the average customer order by 10 percent or more. Kiosks also effectively hide the line. This is important, because customers who see a line of people waiting to place an order will often change their mind and go elsewhere.[4]

All this automation provides another advantage to fast food franchises. Companies like McDonald's make the bulk of their revenue from renting real estate and selling products and services to franchise operators. Automation is another thing it can sell to the businesses operating its restaurants. Franchise operators are willing to invest in automation because it reduces their labor costs and makes their operation more consistent.

Frontline customer service employees are right to worry about losing their jobs. Fast food franchises have a financial incentive to invest in more automation, and automation appears to be cheaper and better than using employees to take orders.

Fortunately, that's an illusion. Fast food chains leading the charge on automation are struggling with customer satisfaction. McDonald's ranked last out of 13 major fast food chains in Intouch Insight's 2025 drive-thru study. Taco Bell ranked 10th. Wendy's came in 8th.[5] The company that came in first wins with human service.

The impact of warm greetings

Chick-fil-A is different.

While the company does use some automation, it uses humanity to gain a competitive advantage. The chain ranked first in friendliness in the Intouch Insight study. That friendliness rating helped it earn the top spot for overall satisfaction, despite ranking last in drive-thru speed and seventh in order accuracy.

You're likely to be greeted by a friendly human standing next to your car when you pull in to the drive-thru at Chick-fil-A. They smile, make eye contact, and greet you in a naturally friendly way.

Step inside a Chick-fil-A, and a human cashier will take your order. Like their drive-thru counterparts, they consistently smile, make eye contact, and serve you with genuine friendliness.

Those greetings are just the tip of the iceberg. Chick-fil-A does a lot of things well. They offer good food and have clean, welcoming restaurants. A friendly human greeting sets the tone for the rest of the experience.

Chick-fil-A's advantage extends beyond just customer satisfaction. The chain earns an estimated 87 percent more revenue per store than McDonald's and 248 percent more revenue per store than Wendy's or Taco Bell.[6] Those results are even more impressive when you consider that Chick-fil-A is closed on Sundays, giving it one less operating day per week than the other chains.

Greeting customers is a standard in nearly every customer service environment. Restaurant employees welcome guests. Retail employees greet customers and offer assistance. Contact center agents start every conversation with a greeting. Why do we do it?

There's a practical aspect. A greeting can tell a customer that an employee is available to serve them. And though most customers would prefer "Hello" or "Welcome," that fast food cashier yelling "Next!" served this purpose.

Greeting customers is a service standard for many companies. Transactional employees greet customers merely to comply with corporate rules. Humans understand there's another reason to greet customers.

A good greeting makes customers feel welcome. It gets customers to let down their guard. They become more optimistic about their service experience, which makes them easier and more enjoyable to serve.

Setting the right tone is critical. Customers often carry a lot of negative emotions with them. They worry about being late to work when they drop by their local coffee shop. They're frustrated about traffic or a busy parking lot as they walk into a retail store. They're exhausted from a long, difficult day as they enter a fast food restaurant.

These emotions shape how customers view their experience. A study by Scott Wiltermuth and Larissa Tiedens found that upset people are more judgmental.[7] They're more likely to nitpick minor service issues.

Research from Maurice Schweitzer and Francesca Gino discovered that angry people are less open to ideas.[8] A frustrated customer is more likely to reject an offer of assistance or react negatively to the solution an employee proposes.

A good greeting can completely change a customer's demeanor. You can see the change. They start smiling. Their body language relaxes and becomes more open. The customer slows down and faces the employee, human to human.

Alaska Airlines is my preferred airline. They consistently rank at or near the top of customer service rankings for U.S. carriers. One thing that stands out is how passengers are greeted as they board the plane.

Gate agents consistently welcome passengers with a smile and use their first name. "Welcome aboard, Jeff!" Walk down the jetway, and a smiling flight attendant greets you as you board. It sets the tone for a pleasant flight.

I sometimes have to fly a rival airline. Its gate agents rarely smile, make eye contact, or even bother to say "Hello" as they scan my boarding pass. Flight attendants are often equally reluctant to greet passengers. I sometimes play a game to see if I can greet employees first and get them to smile and greet me back.

Companies like Alaska Airlines, Chick-fil-A, and National Car Rental win in part because employees consistently offer authentic human greetings. They put customers at ease and turn routine transactions into pleasant encounters.

What exactly makes a good greeting good? I wanted to find out, so I conducted a field study, observing employee greetings to see what type of greeting made the biggest impact.

How to greet customers

The field study was conducted at four coffee shop locations that are part of a large chain. The chain was an ideal place to observe greetings, because it had a high volume of customers and a predictable pattern of customer interactions. Customers were a mix of drive-thru, people picking up orders placed via the mobile app, and customers placing an order at the cash register.

The chain has service standards for greeting customers. Employees are expected to welcome customers as they enter the store and cashiers are expected to greet customers as they approach the counter to place their order. My research tested whether those service standards were being followed and how customers responded.

I found a seat in each coffee shop with clear views of the front door, the mobile order pick-up counter, and the cash register. My observations were limited to people entering the store, which included people walking in to pick up a mobile order and customers placing an order with the cashier. I observed 401 customer interactions across the four locations.

Employee greetings were uneven despite the coffee chain's stated service standards. Only 48 percent of customers were greeted as they entered the store. Just 65 percent of those greetings were delivered with a smile. Many greetings were so transactional that they made little to no impact on customer demeanor.

Cashiers were more consistent, with 86 percent of customers receiving a greeting as they approached to place their order. However, cashiers were worse at smiling than their coworkers at the door, with just 55 percent of cashiers smiling as they greeted a customer. This wasn't due to a few grouchy cashiers bringing down the average. Every cashier I observed smiled at some customers, but not others. Their smiles disappeared when they became busy or distracted.

Giving customers a warm greeting is an expectation in nearly every business. Most customer service professionals I talk to are convinced they are great at greeting customers. Yet the data shows it doesn't happen consistently.

My primary goal was to learn what type of greeting made the biggest impact. I judged this in two ways. Did the customer return the employee's greeting? And did the greeting positively affect the customer's demeanor?

The least effective greeting was when an employee would call out, "Welcome!" the instant a customer walked through the door. It was mildly disorienting to the customer, who often wasn't sure where the greeting was coming from or whether they were the person be-ing greeted. Some customers looked around to find the greeter, but couldn't find them because the employee had already turned to other tasks. Just 38 percent of customers returned these greetings, and only 16 percent of those customers smiled.

The most effective greetings followed the 10 and 5 technique, a com-mon standard in hospitality. The employee waited until the customer was within 10 feet, faced the customer, smiled, and made eye contact. They gave the customer a warm verbal greeting once the customer was five feet away.

It was clear to customers that these greetings were directed at them. Most reacted as humans naturally do when they encounter another friendly person. Customers returned 77 percent of 10 and 5 greetings. They smiled 82 percent of the time.

Lei was an employee I observed who provided a great example. She was stationed at her store's mobile pick-up counter, approximately 30 feet from the front door. Lei waited for customers to approach within 10 feet before turning towards the customer, smiling, and making eye contact. She gave the customer a warm verbal greeting, such as "Good morning" or "Welcome" when they were within five feet. You could tell Lei genuinely wanted to make customers feel welcome in her store.

Her greetings had a consistently positive effect. Customers returned Lei's smile. They relaxed their body language, changing from tense and hurried to relaxed and open. Many took a moment to chat with Lei as she helped them find their mobile order, offered them a stopper for their drink lid, or just engaged in friendly conversation.

Observing Lei revealed something unexpected: her friendly greet-ings had a ripple effect throughout the coffee shop. Customers moved more quickly when they were guided by Lei's gentle direction. Fewer customers seemed irritated at having to wait in line because of the friendly atmosphere Lei helped create. The mobile order counter stayed clean and organized, thanks to Lei's careful attention. Orders came out faster because baristas making drinks were freed from the obligation to constantly interrupt their work to greet customers themselves.

I noticed the same thing at other locations. The coffee shop seemed friendlier when an employee like Lei consistently greeted customers using the 10 and 5 technique. Coworkers were more helpful and outgoing. Customers smiled more and slowed down to enjoy their experience.

There are two things that stand out from this research. First, it proved what many customer service professionals already know: a direct, genuinely friendly greeting, delivered with a smile, disarms customers and makes them feel welcome.

The second thing that stood out is how few employees regularly use this very human greeting. A restaurant host barely makes eye contact as they robotically greet guests with, "How many?" A contact center representative exudes despair as they answer phone call after phone call. A retail employee haphazardly throws "You doin' all right?" at customers to check the greeting box on the list of service standards.

There are plenty of reasons why employees don't greet customers properly. Some aren't friendly or truly don't care. Others have succumbed to a toxic culture or have grown tired of working for a bad boss.

Many just don't make good human greetings a priority. Every coffee shop employee I observed greeted some, but not all, customers the right way. They were all clearly capable, just inconsistent.

This shows that a service standard alone isn't enough. Managers need to train employees on the right way to greet customers, coach them to help build their skills, and model the greetings themselves to set a positive example. Operations need adequate staffing to make human greetings possible. Leaders must also create a culture where employees are proud to come to work and greeting customers humanely is natural and effortless.

I was one of those employees who needed training, coaching, and a good boss. My first job was at a retail clothing store. I naturally understood I was supposed to be friendly, but I didn't intuitively know the right way to greet a customer. It was fortunate that I had a good boss who taught me the importance of customer greetings, showed me the right way to do it, and was a consistently positive role model when she was on the sales floor.

You might be surprised to learn my boss frequently had to remind me to smile early on. Far from "forced friendliness," it was a welcome and helpful reminder. I didn't naturally smile when I was concentrating on a task like folding clothes or ringing up a customer's purchase. My boss's helpful coaching reminded me to disengage from tasks and put my attention where it belonged—on the customer.

Greeting regular customers

One more type of greeting stood out in my coffee shop research.

There were employees in each coffee shop who recognized regular customers. The employees and customers greeted each other like old friends, expressing genuine joy and calling each other by name. There weren't any scripts, service standards, or techniques involved. If you're a human, you know how to greet a friend.

That's how Ali greeted me as I became a regular at the Westin Portland. Matt at TrueValue was the same, which made his "What are YOU doing here?" greeting so perfect. You probably have people who greet you like an old friend when you do business in places where you're a regular.

As a keynote speaker, I've had the opportunity to deliver presentations for several clients that own and manage apartment communities. I visited their communities as part of my preparation so I could observe first-hand how employees interacted with residents.

The best employees knew an astonishing number of residents by name. They understood that although they were at work, the residents they served were at home. Greeting the residents they saw each day like old friends was a very human way of making people feel welcome in their communities. That sense of welcome was the number one reason people chose to sign a lease at a particular apartment community and then renew that lease at the end of the term.

One employee, Jennifer, always had dog treats in her pocket. There were many residents in her community who had dogs. Jennifer understood that including dogs in her regular greetings was a natural extension of greeting the dogs' human owners. I observed Jennifer with a group of happy, expectant dogs surrounding her, tails wagging, waiting to be greeted with a treat. The dogs' owners looked on, beaming, as they chatted with Jennifer.

This didn't look like work or a required transaction. It looked like a genuine interaction. The community manager told me it was also a winning strategy. The apartment community was physically no different than other communities in the neighborhood. Like other communities, they had an impressive website where you could get details on each available unit and even take a virtual tour. The process for viewing apartments, scheduling an appointment for a site visit, and even signing a lease were all automated. The apartments themselves were older, but well-maintained. Just like everywhere else in the neighborhood.

What set it apart was employees like Jennifer who made a habit of greeting residents and making them feel welcome. The community boasted higher occupancy and resident retention rates than its competitors because employees consistently nailed the human connection.

Phone greetings

One of the reasons I enjoy flying Alaska Airlines is they have consistently friendly employees. Flight crews, gate agents, and customer service reps make the travel experience better.

Occasionally, I have to call the airline for help with my travel plans, and I always get a fantastic greeting.

"Hi, this is Becky in Boise. Who do I have the pleasure of speaking with?"

I instantly feel myself relax when I'm connected with Becky in Boise, Tony in Tucson, Sarah in Seattle, or whoever answers the phone. It starts the call with can-do energy that makes me feel this person is on my side and happy to help me.

The greeting seems so simple, but there's a lot of goodness packed into these two short sentences. Let's break it down a bit.

It starts before an employee even answers the phone. Alaska's reservation and customer care numbers are easy to find. They're on their website and in the app. Many companies frustrate customers by making them go on an irritating phone number scavenger hunt.

Alaska makes it easy to connect with a human. The company understands that most passengers are calling because they either tried self-service and it didn't work for them, or they want the extra confidence of having a helpful human guide them.

Other companies use a number of techniques to avoid having you talk to a live customer service agent even after you dial their number. It's known as call deflection. Strategies include swamping you with endless phone menus, forcing you to deal with an AI voice agent that tries to solve your issue before connecting you, and making you wait on hold until you're exhausted.

Not at Alaska Airlines. Wait times are minimal. There are few digital barriers. You get connected to Becky in Boise in no time.

Alaska employees consistently answer the phone with genuine friendliness. They avoid the robotic tones so many phone agents use or the fake enthusiasm a few inject into their greeting. The call starts with someone who immediately sounds like they want to help.

The greeting itself works well because it's simple. The employee says "Hi," offers their name and location, and then asks for your name.

Asking for the customer's name up front is already an invitation to begin building rapport. I naturally find myself responding with "Hi, Becky. I'm Jeff."

"Hi, Jeff," says Becky. "How may I help you today?"

The experience stands out because it's so different from the usual greetings you get when calling customer service. Many customer service agents are given clunky required greetings that were dreamed up by someone who'd never spent a day answering customer calls. Here's a real example:

"Thank you for calling (company), where every day is a great and wonderful day. My name is (name). How can I make your day great and wonderful today?"

There's no way you could say that mouthful of nonsense and sound like a human. It screams inauthenticity. Real people don't talk like that.

Some customer service teams skip phone greetings entirely. Agents instead answer the phone by issuing a curt command for the customer to provide information. "Customer service, may I have your full name and date of birth?" It's nearly impossible for customer service reps to build any kind of rapport when the call starts that way.

You don't have to copy the greeting used at Alaska Airlines. What matters is that you find a greeting that puts *your* callers at ease and allows you to quickly connect with them on a human level.

Practice: Your best phone greeting

I've worked in contact centers as a frontline agent, trainer, manager, and consultant. I know how hard it is to give customers a great greeting on your 50th call of the day. It gets worse when something's happened that causes a lot of those customers to be upset.

There are two techniques that can help.

The first is to calibrate your perfect greeting. Listen to past calls or record yourself answering the phone. Try to find a clear and simple way to answer the phone with just the right amount of genuine warmth. You don't want to sound like a robot or as if you're forcing enthusiasm. The goal is to make the caller feel welcome.

Your customer can't see you, but your body language still influences how friendly you sound. Try adjusting your body language by sitting up with good, comfortable posture, and smile as you answer the phone. I like to pretend the customer is sitting right in front of me so it's easier to remember to answer the phone with genuine friendliness.

Keep practicing even after you've found your perfect greeting. Set an intention to use it on every call. The more you do it, the easier it becomes. A good greeting should sound and feel effortless.

The second technique is to do a quick mental reset between calls. A difficult call can stay in your mind and influence your mood as you transition to the next one. A mental reset helps clear out the last call so you can refocus on giving the next customer a great greeting.

Here's how to do a quick mental reset:

1. Take a deep breath
2. Smile
3. Focus on clearing your mind

Try it now. You'll likely feel an instant positive shift in your mood. This technique takes just a couple of seconds, but it can clear out any lingering annoyance and prime you to answer your next call with genuine friendliness.

Let's recap

An authentic human greeting makes people feel welcome. It relaxes customers and makes them receptive to a great experience.

Companies that excel at customer greetings consistently outperform the competition. Chick-fil-A leads the fast food industry by leaning into humans greeting customers at the drive-thru and in the dining room. Alaska Airlines stands out among airlines by greeting customers with true friendliness, including those who call the company's phone lines. National Car Rental leads the rental car industry by using excellent automation for mundane tasks while having friendly employees who greet customers with genuine human kindness when customers need help.

The way you greet customers makes a big difference. Direct, simple, and friendly greetings consistently work the best.

Use the 10 and 5 approach for in-person greetings. When a customer approaches within 10 feet, turn toward them, make eye contact, and smile. Offer a friendly verbal greeting once they're within five feet.

Short, simple greetings work best on the phone. Record yourself practicing your greeting until you find one that effortlessly makes customers feel welcome.

Greeting customers is just the first step toward making a powerful connection. In the next chapter, we'll explore ways that building rapport can make a difference.

CHAPTER 2 NOTES

1   "Starbucks Reports Q4 and Full Fiscal Year 2024 Results," Starbucks website, accessed October 30, 2024, https://investor.starbucks.com/news/financial-releases/news-details/2024/Starbucks-Reports-Q4-and-Full-Fiscal-Year-2024-Results/default.aspx.

2   "11 QSR Chains Using AI Drive-Thru Technology (and What Could Go Wrong)," Canopy website, accessed October 14, 2025, https://www.gocanopy.com/news-insights/ai-drive-thru-problems.

3   Isabelle Bousquette, "McDonald's Gives Its Restaurants an AI Makeover," (*The Wall Street Journal*, March 5, 2025).

4   "Should Fast-Food Chains Fully Commit to Digital Kiosks?" (*RetailWire*, April 3, 2024).

5   InTouch Insight, "25th Annual Intouch Insight Drive-Thru Study," (October 6, 2025).

6   QSR, "QSR 50 2025: Top 50 Fast-Food Chains, Ranked by Sales," (August 1, 2025). Chick-fil-A's revenue numbers are estimated since the company is privately held.

7   Scott S. Wiltermuth, Larissa Z. Tiedens, "Incidental anger and the desire to evaluate," (*Organizational Behavior and Human Decision Processes*, Volume 116, Issue 1, September 2011, Pages 55-65), doi:10.1016/J.OBHDP.2011.03.007.

8   Francesca Gino and Maurice E. Schweitzer, "Blinded by Anger or Feeling the Love: How Emotions Influence Advice Taking," (*Journal of Applied Psychology*, Vol. 93, No. 5, 2008, Pages 1165–1173), doi:10.1037/0021-9010.93.5.1165.

CHAPTER THREE
Rapport

GIL GREETED PASSENGERS AS THEY STEPPED onto the tram on a crisp fall evening. The tram was perched at the top of the mountain, ready to take 30 people on a 10-minute ride down to the valley 6,000 feet below.

The last passenger stepped in, and Gil closed the tram doors. He made a few safety announcements over the tram's public address system as the tram left the boarding station and slipped into the night to begin its descent.

The only sounds were the gentle mountain breeze coming through the tram's open windows and the low hum of people talking quietly in the darkened tram cabin. Then Gil turned on some music.

The crowd's murmur stopped as the music caught people's attention. The first line confirmed the song was "Sweet Caroline" as Neil Diamond's voice came through the tram speakers.

"Sing it if you know it," Gil said over the tram's PA system. A few people began to sing. More started singing as the song moved towards the chorus. And then it became contagious.

"Everybody!" shouted Gil. The entire tram car erupted as 30 strangers joyously belted out the chorus. "Sweet Caroline! (Bum bum bum!)"

Gil followed the first song with another popular hit. Passengers kept singing. A few added dance moves in the confined space of the tram. The short ride seemed even shorter.

The tram passengers were abuzz by the time they arrived at the base of the mountain. People were smiling and laughing. Strangers complimented each other's voices. Many were disappointed that the ride had ended so soon.

Gil had created a moment. He did it by using the power of human connection to build genuine rapport with and between his passengers, encouraging them to spread good humor and fun.

You'd be forgiven for thinking this tram ride was a special one. It certainly was for the passengers onboard, but Gil uses these techniques to create moments like this several times a night for each tram load of people he brings down the mountain.

The *Merriam-Webster* dictionary defines rapport as "a friendly, harmonious relationship, especially: a relationship characterized by agreement, mutual understanding, or empathy that makes communication possible or easy."[1] This definition provides important clues about what makes rapport genuine and why it's so essential in customer service.

Rapport is a process of getting customers to know, like, and trust you so you can serve them better. You can observe genuine rapport in the way a customer reacts to an employee. They smile, begin using more open body language, and the tone of the conversation sounds cooperative. Some even sing.

In this chapter, we'll explore the impact of genuine rapport on your customers' experiences. I'll share specific techniques you can use to make authentic human connections with the people you serve.

But first, let's talk about what happens when attempts to build rapport are stilted, forced, and insincere.

Why insincere rapport backfires

Gil excels at building genuine rapport with the passengers riding on his tram.

A cynic might wonder if everything Gil does is an act. It's not. He truly enjoys making his passengers' experience a memorable one. That sincere intent to build rapport is the most important characteristic of what makes rapport genuine. Humans can tell whether someone truly means it, or they're just going through the motions.

You've seen disingenuous attempts at rapport. Employees say "Welcome" with the enthusiasm of gray paint. They use your name like they're working through a checklist. (They are.) They ask questions like "How are you today?" without really caring about the answer. It feels transactional.

Acting like a robot won't get customers to know, like, and trust you. These phony rapport tactics make the experience worse, not better. Customers instinctively put up their guard, eying the offending employee with suspicion. Insincere rapport is friction for customers. It slows them down and makes the experience uncomfortable.

This was a lesson I learned the hard way. My first job was working in a retail clothing store. One of the store's service standards was for employees to greet every customer who walked into their department.

I thought I was doing well by greeting every customer with, "How's it going?" Most customers acknowledged my greeting and said, "Fine." It went well for the first few days.

One day, a customer responded to my greeting with, "Terrible!" I stood in stunned silence, not knowing what to say. The standard response up until then had always been "Fine."

The customer saw my hesitation and added, "Well, you asked!"

It was a lesson I never forgot. She was right to call me out. I had asked how she was doing without actually caring about the answer.

From that day forward, I made it my mission to only ask customers questions when I wanted to know the answer. It prepared me for the next time I asked a customer how they were doing and they said they were having a bad day. That time, I was able to pause and empathize with the customer. "I'm sorry to hear your day isn't going so well, but I'm glad you're here now. Is there anything I can do to make it better?" The customer appreciated my sincere attempt to build rapport and be helpful.

That experience helped me realize just how many employees ask customers rapport-building questions without caring about the answer. Scripted speech without care or feeling is more annoying than useful.

Cashiers routinely ask, "Did you find everything okay?" as they ring up your purchases. Watch what happens if you tell them, "No." Most stop and stare at you because they have no idea how to respond. The expected answer is always, "Yes."

These insincere questions make customers feel disconnected from the people serving them. They like employees less, not more. Even worse, it can feel like an intrusion.

I occasionally have to go into my bank and interact with a teller. Their half-hearted attempts at rapport are predictable. On Mondays, the teller always asks, "How was your weekend?" On Tuesdays, Wednesdays, and Thursdays, the question changes to "How's your day going so far?" Fridays, the question of the day becomes "Any plans for the weekend?"

The answer doesn't matter. You could reply to the Monday question with "I won the lottery," or "My house burned down," and you'd likely get the same tepid, uncaring response. "That's great." The teller is just dutifully asking the question of the day while they pull up my account and work through the transaction.

This is where automation has an advantage over automatons. The bank's app, website, and in-branch ATM machines don't try to build phony rapport. They don't pepper you with meaningless questions about your day. The automation processes your transaction quickly and efficiently without all the insipid small talk. Customers use automation because it's convenient and because they don't have to interact with a transactional person doing their best robot impersonation.

The customers who still go inside and wait for a teller typically do so because they lack confidence using automation or require assistance that automation can't easily provide. I occasionally receive a physical check from a client. I always use a teller to deposit it because the ATM machine has mishandled my deposit on more than one occasion and the bank's app-based deposit feature doesn't work for my account.

I once had all my personal and business accounts at this bank. The lack of human service combined with broken automation caused me to switch banks for my personal banking needs. I've kept my business accounts there because I so rarely need to go into a branch, but I'm always mildly annoyed at having to endure the tellers' forced banter.

Customers bristle at insincerity. Many tell me they'd rather be left alone than accosted by an employee wearing a fake smile who pretends to care about them. It's obviously performative and feels awkward.

I saw the impact of insincerity while sitting in coffee shops observing employees for my employee greeting study (see Chapter Two).

Insincere greetings barely moved the needle. Most customers never smiled, and many didn't bother to return the employee's greeting. They just plowed ahead on their mission to get in, get coffee, and get out.

Simply giving customers a genuine smile made them more likely to return a greeting. Just 25 percent of customers returned an employee's greeting when the employee didn't smile at them. Most just walked past on their mission to get caffeine. However, the number of customers who returned an employee greeting tripled to 76 percent when the employee smiled.

The goal of rapport is to get customers to know, like, and trust you. Fake rapport does the opposite. Customers like you less. They try to avoid interactions. And they certainly don't trust your intentions.

How automation influences rapport

In October 2019, I decided to run a small experiment when I travelled to Seattle, Washington. I would try to rely entirely on automation throughout the trip.

My plane ticket and hotel stay were both purchased online. I used the airline's app to check in for my flight and generate a boarding pass. At the airport, I had marginal human contact with the TSA agent as I passed through the security checkpoint, and again at the gate as a human scanned my digital boarding pass. The flight featured a bit more human interaction since I was flying Alaska Airlines; their flight attendants are always friendly.

Everything was automated once I arrived in Seattle. I bought a ticket for the light rail at the airport kiosk and boarded a train into the city. It was a short walk from the train station to the hotel, where I checked in on the hotel's mobile app. The app created a mobile key that allowed me to bypass the front counter and go straight to my room.

It was soon time to head out and explore the city. The Lyft app summoned a vehicle and tracked my ride the entire way. I used the app to rate the friendly driver (five stars!), pay for the ride, and leave a tip with just a few clicks. Admittedly, I broke character for a moment and chatted with my driver during the ride. I just couldn't help myself.

I wanted coffee. The Starbucks app helped me find a nearby location, order my drink, and pay for it. I walked into the store a few minutes later and my hot coffee was waiting for me on the counter. I picked it up and left without even an acknowledgment from an employee.

When I got hungry, I walked to a nearby Amazon Go store. I entered using the Amazon Go app, selected some snacks from the shelves, and left the store without ever having to talk to anyone. The store used AI to track my movements and identify the items I took with me. The app automatically calculated my purchases.

It was all pretty amazing. It was also a little lonely and surreal to travel with such minimal human interaction, even though it felt wonderfully efficient.

These were all situations where human employees don't routinely add uniquely human value. Buying an airline ticket, booking a hotel room, or getting a ticket for the light rail all used to require interacting with a person. Now it's faster and easier to do it via an app or kiosk. Seattle's light rail system has a tap-to-pay feature where you can tap your chipped credit or debit card at the turnstile to pay your fare without even stopping at the ticket machine. It's so much easier!

You can use an app to buy coffee or order food for delivery without ever having to interact with another human being. The coffee is waiting on the counter when you arrive. The food is left on your doorstep. You can walk into many stores and use self-checkout, ensuring you never have to deal with a cashier.

AI takes this automation to a new level. You can use AI to help you pick out a new jacket when you accidentally leave your old one in the back of a rental car. AI can help you plan a road trip, evaluate insurance policies, or get roadside assistance if your vehicle breaks down. All of that used to require humans with varying degrees of helpfulness. AI makes it fast and easy without the small talk or the unnecessary waiting.

AI is driving all sorts of helpful automation that makes the customer journey easier. Car dealerships use AI to answer calls and route them to the appropriate person. Medical clinics use AI to automatically send patients appointment reminders, prompt them to complete necessary paperwork, and share test results. Credit card companies use AI to detect fraud and automatically alert customers about potential issues.

Rapport doesn't add any value to most of these interactions. You don't need connection to make a purchase, get a reservation, or fill out some paperwork—you just need to get it done. Most customers would rather get instant service than wait for a human to be available.

Transactional employees stand out like a sore thumb when self-service automation works well. Why wait in line for cold, uncaring service from a person when you can get instant service from a cold, uncaring robot? Employees only make sense when they can add human value.

I once checked into an airport hotel that had once been a working airport terminal. The hotel had preserved many historical aspects and incorporated them into the design. I'd travelled through this building several times as a kid when it was an airport terminal, so I was excited to visit. Guests were directed to the original airline check-in counters to check in to the hotel. The hotel was really leaning into the theme!

Check-in was done via a self-service kiosk. There was an employee standing behind the kiosk as I approached, and I hoped to ask him a few questions about the property. Engaging with guests apparently wasn't part of his job because he was staring at his phone as I approached, and he never looked up even when I smiled and said, "Hello."

I started the check-in process and noticed he still hadn't looked up. I asked a question about the hotel out loud to no one in particular, and he still didn't look up. Yes, that was passive-aggressive, but it was also amusing as I was now on a mission to see what would get this employee to respond, since saying hello and standing right in front of him hadn't worked.

The employee steadfastly refused to engage even as I completed the check-in and retrieved my room key. At this point, I went for one last move and got out my phone to take a selfie with my newest "friend." The picture turned out great, with me smiling at the camera and the hotel employee obliviously playing with his phone.

If this is what employees bring to service, who needs them? Automation is cheaper, more efficient, and more enjoyable for customers than transactional people posing as automatons.

Genuine rapport isn't needed for every customer interaction, but it has an important place. It's necessary when customers need someone they can trust to give them advice or help solve a tricky problem. It's welcome when it adds obvious value.

The impact of genuine rapport

There's a tire store in my neighborhood that has a 3.7-star rating on Yelp. That rating skyrockets to 4.9 when you control for one variable: whether the review mentions an employee by name.

Reviews that mention an employee by name are almost always five stars. These reviews elevate the store's overall average, which helps it attract new customers. The positive reviews also signal that many customers remain loyal, despite experiencing issues, because of the efforts of one or more employees.

Customers are more likely to learn an employee's name when they make a genuine connection. Here are some of the comments from five-star reviews about the tire shop:

- "Doug arranged a free patch for me. Super appreciated his kindness!"
- "Mike at the front was very responsive and even followed up the next day."
- "It was a rainy day and they were busy, but Jesse told me that he really wanted to help me."

Customers tend to dehumanize employees in negative reviews. Notice the difference from these one-star comments about the same store:

- "They asked me to drop it off and gave a bad vibe."
- "They were completely unprofessional in the way they handled everything."
- "I was placed on hold for 5 minutes, listening to him heavily breathing like he had just run a marathon."

There's another tire store next to this one. It has a 4.5-star Yelp rating. One explanation is that it has more reviews mentioning an employee by name (60% vs. 48%) than the store with a 3.7-star rating. This store's employees are more adept at consistently building rapport.

I've replicated this research many times. Online reviews and customer surveys that mention employees by name consistently have higher average ratings than those that don't name an employee. Digging deeper, these employees stand out because they build genuine rapport with the customers they serve. They do something that makes them memorable—the kind of human a customer wants to know by name. This leads to greater customer loyalty and a better reputation.

I first noticed it when analyzing survey data for a client. A survey that mentioned an employee by name was much more likely to give a high satisfaction rating than a survey where no employee was mentioned. Many of those surveys contain constructive comments about aspects of the experience customers thought could be improved, yet they still gave a top overall mark and mentioned a particular employee who had made a difference.

Several employees were mentioned more than others in the surveys. I spent time observing their interactions with customers and quickly understood why they stood out. They took a sincere interest in each customer they served. You could tell they weren't just going through a service checklist as they helped each person. They treated people with humanity.

My client's management team shared the findings about names appearing in surveys with their employees. Some employees misconstrued the intent and began making a concerted effort to get mentioned by name in a survey without actually trying to build rapport. Customers saw through those insincere efforts, and those survey scores barely budged.

Genuine rapport helps customers know, like, and trust you. This is a recipe for a great overall experience. Customers relax. They're more open to help and suggestions from employees. Liking the people who are serving them makes customers more forgiving of mistakes.

The key to it all is that rapport must be authentic. You can't fake connection or mandate it with a clunky corporate script. It has to be real.

It took some extra work for my client to get everyone back on track and help employees realize that just getting named in a survey was no replacement for genuine rapport. It was merely an indicator. I helped my client identify specific skills and techniques employees could use to create stronger connections with the people they served and incorporate them into their customer-service training.

The end goal isn't getting named in a survey. Instead, it's creating such a strong connection with a customer that they naturally remember who you are. That connection is different with every customer you serve. There isn't a single approach that works well with everyone.

I once ran an experiment with contact center agents to see how various factors affected their efficiency, including rapport. Agents were asked to "read" the customer at the start of the call and adjust their approach based on their perception of the customer's intentions. When a customer was in a hurry, they kept rapport to a minimum and worked quickly. They slowed down and spent more time building rapport when a customer was in a good mood or seemed to want extra attention.

Customers were happier when agents adjusted to their needs. And surprisingly, the average call length *decreased* when agents adapted their approach to each individual customer! Agents saved time by avoiding unnecessary rapport-building with customers who clearly didn't want it. That allowed them to spend more time building rapport with customers who appreciated it, while still saving time overall.

The experiment revealed a big lesson about genuine rapport: part of what makes it genuine is adjusting your approach to every customer you serve.

How to build genuine rapport

Rapport is a human skill. It comes easily when you spend time with someone you genuinely like.

Think about a time when you met someone and just instantly clicked. You immediately knew this person was a friend. Smiling was natural. You faced each other with open body language, unconsciously leaning in to create a stronger connection. Your tone was warm and animated, and you laughed easily. An observer would be able to tell you and your new friend were genuinely interested in what each other had to say.

Those are the same skills you can use to build genuine rapport with customers.

- Intention
- Congruency
- Interest

It starts with intent—you have to truly want to create a positive connection. Customers can spot a phony a mile away.

Intention is a skill because it requires you to block out distractions and focus your energy on the customer you're serving. Distraction is a challenge that makes rapport more difficult.

When I did that field study in coffee shops, I found that customers were greeted only 48 percent of the time as they entered a store. Of those greetings, just 65 percent were delivered with a smile.

The problem was obvious: baristas were distracted. They were expected to make drinks as quickly as possible, while also stopping what they were doing to greet customers as they entered the store. The result was baristas calling out "Welcome!" as a customer entered while they continued to work. It was a flat, ineffective greeting.

Those same employees often smiled when they greeted a customer in between tasks. Being distraction-free allowed them to focus on the customer and offer a more friendly and genuine greeting.

The second skill is congruency. This means your words, tone, and body language all match your intent to create a positive connection. Saying "Welcome" to a customer with a monotone voice and a scowl on your face sends mixed signals. On the other hand, "Welcome" delivered in a warm tone with a smile and friendly eye contact is likely to make a customer feel truly welcome.

Psychologist Albert Mehrabian conducted a series of experiments to show the impact of congruence on likability. He found that people are more likable when their words, tone, and body language all send the same message. Mehrabian's research revealed that body language carries the most weight when our words, tone, and body language send conflicting messages.[2]

He estimated how much each contributed to likability when the words, tone, and body language don't match.

- 55 percent body language
- 38 percent tone of voice
- 7 percent words

It's important to note that this research has been misconstrued by many customer service trainers to mean that **all communication** neatly falls into these percentages. That's not the case at all.

Mehrabian's research focused specifically on **likability** and the impact when people's words, tone, and body language all sent the same or different messages.

Burnout is common in customer service work, and it has an unsurprisingly negative impact on an employee's natural desire to smile or communicate in a warm tone of voice. I did a study involving nearly 1,000 contact center agents and found that 59 percent were at risk of burnout. An employee's burnout risk increased dramatically when they felt they weren't empowered to serve customers, they weren't paid fairly for their work, and their boss wasn't supportive. For those employees, the best path to smiling again might be finding a job that's a better cultural fit.[3]

Some employees try to fake a smile, but customers can see the difference in your eyes. Psychologist Paul Ekman studied real and fake smiles to map facial movements and identify the specific markers of genuine and fake smiles. A real smile causes the cheeks to pull up and the skin below the eye may bag or bulge. The lower eyelid moves up and crows-feet wrinkles may appear. The skin above the eye pulls slightly down and inwards.[4]

Fake smiles look similar to real smiles at the mouth, but the eyes are different. They don't have the same muscle movement around the eyes that occurs when someone is smiling for real.

The third skill is to demonstrate genuine interest in your customers. Your true desire to be helpful will shine through if you actually care about the people you serve.

The Five Question technique can make building genuine rapport easier. It works by thinking of five questions you might use to break the ice with a customer, get them talking about themselves, and learn a little more about their needs. Having five different questions at the ready makes it easier to select just one in any given situation.

I speak at a lot of conferences, and I spend time networking with attendees and meeting new people when I attend these events. The Five Question technique makes it easy. Here are the questions I prepared before a conference for contact center professionals.

1. What brings you to this conference?

2. Have you been to one of these conferences before?

3. Is there a particular challenge you hope to solve while you're here?

4. What's your connection to the contact center industry?

5. What are you most looking forward to at the conference?

The answers to these questions made it easier for me to take a genuine interest in the many new people I met at the event. For example, one person told me they came to the conference because their team was a finalist for an industry award. They beamed when I congratulated them and asked about the best practices that earned the team their spot in the finals.

You can use this same technique in nearly any industry. Create a list of questions to break the ice and learn more about your customers. Try to go behind the rote questions my local bank uses. "How was your weekend?" is pleasant, but it doesn't reveal much about your customer's needs.

A restaurant server might ask, "Have you dined with us before?" First-time guests might appreciate a brief overview of the menu. A returning guest might appreciate being welcomed back.

A retail associate might ask, "What brings you in today?" Knowing the customer's mission makes it easier to offer them assistance. The customer could also say, "I'm just looking" if they just want to be left alone to browse.

Finally, it's very human to introduce yourself by name. That's how we meet people in nearly any other social context. Offering your name to a customer and making the effort to learn theirs breaks the ice and makes the interaction more personal.

Let's recap

Customers appreciate genuine rapport when it adds to their experience.

Phony rapport detracts from the experience. It slows customers down and makes people uncomfortable. Seamless automation is often a better experience than a transactional person who merely pretends to care.

Genuine rapport helps customers feel more comfortable. It lightens customers' moods and makes communication easier.

1. **Intention:** start with an intent to care.

2. **Congruency:** use consistent body language, tone, and words.

3. **Interest:** take a genuine interest in each customer you serve.

Try using the Five Question technique to think of a list of rapport-building questions you can try with your customers. Experiment with each question and observe how your customer reacts.

In the next chapter, we'll move from connecting with customers to understanding their needs. That starts with listening.

CHAPTER 3 NOTES

1 *Merriam-Webster.com*, "rapport (n.)," accessed January 11, 2026, https://www.merriam-webster.com/dictionary/rapport.

2 Albert Mehrabian, *Silent Messages*, (Wadsworth Publishing Company, January 1, 1972).

3 The author's complete burnout study can be accessed at https://toistersolutions.com/burnout.

4 Paul Ekman, "The importance of the Duchenne smile," Paul Ekman Group website, accessed January 11, 2026, https://www.paulekman.com/blog/fake-smile-or-genuine-smile.

SECTION TWO:

Understanding

Listening

ONE THING YOU NEVER WANT TO hear a flight attendant say as you board a plane is "Oh, shit!"

The airline caterer was at the door directly opposite where I was entering. There was a small pop as he opened the door to access the forward galley, and something moved at the bottom of the door.

The flight attendant had forgotten to deactivate the emergency evacuation slide. Opening the door had activated it. She realized the enormity of her mistake and blurted, "Oh, shit!"

There were two disappointments. First, the catering truck was blocking the slide so it couldn't fully deploy. It just popped out of its case a few inches before getting stopped by the catering truck. It would've been fun to see the slide completely inflated on the side of the plane.

The second disappointment was that it put the plane out of service. You can't just tuck the slide back in the case and get on with the flight. Whatever the airline needed to do to fix it wasn't going to happen that night in Cleveland. The plane was now broken and everyone had to get off.

My original itinerary was to fly from Cleveland to Dallas and catch a connecting flight home to San Diego. Now I worried whether I could get to San Diego that night, and where I was going to stay if the airline couldn't get me home.

There were multiple variables to consider. Could I get to Dallas in time to catch a later flight to San Diego? Were there routes through other cities that would get me home? Where was I going to spend the night if I couldn't get home? Did it make more sense to stay in Cleveland, or fly part way home and stay the night in Dallas?

I needed the airline to help me sort it out and provide hotel and meal vouchers if I was spending the night somewhere other than home.

I tried using the airline's app to search for options, but there was nothing useful. The app was good at routine tasks like booking a flight or retrieving a boarding pass, but there wasn't an option for "flight attendant broke the plane and now I can't get home."

Years ago, the airline was pretty good on social media. I once sent a single Twitter direct message after a canceled flight and 15 minutes later got rebooked on a different routing that got me to my destination in time for a client meeting. Those days are long gone, and that team no longer responds.

Calling was useless. A message informed me that call volume was significantly higher than usual. Perhaps the approximately 150 other passengers on my flight had swamped the phone lines.

There was an option to connect with a live agent via text. I sent a message, explained my predicament, and asked for my options. The agent was an automaton, a transactional person who couldn't understand my needs or present a viable solution. The best they could do was rebook me on a flight leaving the following day, but they weren't able to give me a hotel voucher or advise me on the fastest routing option.

Those failed attempts at service left me just one choice. I joined the long line of passengers from my flight waiting to speak to the lone gate agent. Apparently, the airline hadn't staffed up for an accidental broken plane situation.

Deep breath. I'll probably write a book about this.

Michael was the gate agent. I looked on for 30 minutes as he took the full force of every passenger's emotions. A passenger was worried about missing a job interview. Another was going to be late for a wedding. One person was sobbing because she was going to miss a funeral.

Each passenger had a unique story and a different set of wants and needs. They were all worried about finding a solution. Michael listened to them, one at a time, and tried to understand their needs so he could help.

When it was finally my turn, Michael quickly got what the airline's app and texting bot-person couldn't grasp. He heard what help I was asking for, understood that my intent was to get home as quickly as possible, and empathized with the frustration of a disrupted trip.

Michael advised me to fly to Dallas on the replacement plane that would arrive in three hours. I could spend the night there using the airline's hotel voucher and then catch an early flight home to San Diego.

Michael used uniquely human skills to help a plane-load of passengers that evening. He listened carefully to each person's story and helped sort out a complex array of options to find the best solution. He succeeded where automation and automatons failed because he could hear more than just the words each passenger said. Michael understood their intent.

In this chapter, we'll explore reasons why listening is an underrated skill, how AI plays a role in listening to customers, how humans have an advantage over automaton people when it comes to listening, and specific techniques you can use to become a super-listener.

For the sake of simplicity, I'll use "listening" to mean understanding the needs a customer is trying to communicate, whether verbally or in writing.

Listening is an underrated skill

Think of the most amazing customer service stories you've heard.

Those stories all focus on the customer's predicament and the wonderful things an employee did. But the employee would never have been able to take those wonderful actions without first listening.

Michael shined in a moment of need because of his listening skills. He listened at a level, for a length of time, and to a quantity of customers, that's rare in customer service.

There's a shortage of customer service employees who can listen the way Michael did. It's become normal to encounter automatons who don't make much effort to understand your needs. That type of service is even more frustrating than an actual robot. You expect humans to at least *try* to understand.

I once bought tickets to attend a soccer match with friends. The ticketing app has a feature that allows you to electronically transfer a ticket to someone else. It generates a text message with a link to the ticket so your friend can easily add the ticket to the app on their own phone. The feature wasn't working when I tried to send my friends their tickets. It prompted me to send a text message, but didn't include their ticket link.

There wasn't a self-service solution that fixed the issue, so I contacted a customer service rep via chat. We exchanged quick pleasantries, and then I explained the issue. What followed was a frustrating exchange where the rep couldn't or wouldn't understand the problem.

> **Me:** *"I am trying to transfer tickets via text. The app generates the text message but does not include a link to the ticket."*
>
> **Rep:** *"Upon checking here, I see that you are eligible to transfer for this event. Moreover, I see here that your one ticket under this order is already under a pending transfer which means that your recipient still hasn't accepted the ticket yet."*
>
> **Me:** *"That is incorrect. I'm not able to fully initiate a transfer."*
>
> **Rep:** *"You can check the status of your ticket under your account."*
>
> **Me:** *"Were you able to read the description of the issue I sent? The app generates a text but does not include a link to the ticket."*
>
> **Rep:** *"If you cannot see the status on the App, please try to access your ticket instead using mobile browser."*
>
> **Me:** *"Are you still there?"*
>
> **Rep:** *"Please be advised that the link will be received by your recipient directly through the text message."*
>
> **Me:** *"Please re-read my message."*
>
> **Rep:** *"Did your recipient already see your transfer? Please be advised that after you entered your mobile number, a link to claim the ticket will pop up with a pre-written text message."*

The rep was stuck assuming I didn't know how to transfer a ticket. Try as I might, I couldn't get the rep to understand that the ticket transfer feature wasn't working. The app generated a text message I could send to my friends, but the link to claim the ticket wasn't included in the message.

The problem never got resolved. I had to meet my friends at the stadium gate so I could scan them in using the tickets on my phone.

Misunderstandings like this occur with astounding frequency. They frustrate customers and waste both the customers' and the reps' time. Many issues, like mine, never get resolved.

Ironically, a rush to save time is often the cause of poor listening. Customer service employees are encouraged to work quickly in the name of efficiency. Working faster erodes listening skills. The faster they try to work, the less employees are able to grasp what a customer is trying to tell them.

Distractions also hurt listening skills. The chat rep for the ticketing company was likely engaging with other customers via chat at the same time I was trying to get my issue resolved. Jumping from conversation to conversation creates a natural urge to skip and skim messages, which causes important context and meaning to be lost.

The chat rep also appeared to be using prewritten templates to respond to me. This is a common practice for customer service teams. Unfortunately, using the wrong template or sending a templated message without editing it to better fit the context of the conversation only amplifies the sense that the person isn't listening.

Even humans intent on using their human skills sometimes struggle to fully understand what customers want or need. Customers are notoriously bad at telling their stories. Language barriers can make listening even more challenging. Sometimes, customers ask for what they *think* they need, but what they really need is something else.

Here's a sample challenge. Imagine you work in technical support for an internet service provider and you receive a call from a customer asking for help. What do you think this customer truly needs?

Customer: *"My internet just went down. I need to get it fixed before my client call this afternoon."*

The correct answer often stumps even seasoned customer service professionals. Most people default to the action the customer described—fixing the internet. This is what internet technical support professionals typically focus on as well. They immediately begin walking through routine troubleshooting steps and, if that doesn't work, offer to schedule a technician to go to the customer's home.

That approach is likely to infuriate an anxious customer if the support rep can't get the internet working and a technician needs to be scheduled. The customer mentioned the real issue: their upcoming client call. That call is the reason they need their internet fixed quickly, but it's easy to miss. This solution lands with a thud when the technician isn't available to come to the home and fix the problem before the call.

It takes a savvy listener to recognize that being able to take the client call is the customer's most pressing need. The rep will need to look for options if the internet can't be fixed remotely, such as sharing a list of local Wi-Fi hot spots so the customer can find an alternative location to hold their call.

AI has helped improve human listening in some ways. Contact center agents now use AI-powered software that listens to their phone calls in real time and suggests helpful information and next actions based on the conversation. Despite these advances, there are still significant limitations when it comes to AI understanding customers.

AI struggles with listening

Robots aren't good at listening to complex customer needs.

That's sometimes by design. Raise your hand if you've ever yelled "Human!" into the phone in an attempt to bypass the automated menu and get a real person on the line. Yep, me too.

The company doesn't want to connect you to a human, because humans are more expensive to hire and train than robots. So they make it nearly impossible by programming the AI to ignore your rants. Yell all you want, you're still getting the machine.

Automation sometimes gets confused by a customer's word choice. A bot might not understand "What is the phone number for customer service?" because that department is called "customer support" at this particular company.

AI has made things a little better. Many systems can interpret the different words a customer might use to describe the same thing. It can comprehend that a customer asking for the "customer service" phone number wants to call the customer support team.

Robot listening skills are inconsistent even with AI. Some AI bots are unable to handle the most basic of customer questions, such as "When do you open?" or "Where are you located?" These questions baffle the bot for a number of reasons. Some bots have been poorly designed or trained. Others struggle to reconcile conflicting sources of information. What should the bot reply when the store's website says 9:00 am, but its social media profile says it opens at 10:00?

One area where AI has made leaps and bounds is deciphering complex issues. For example, it's gotten pretty good at handling sticky logistical problems, such as rebooking a plane full of passengers when a flight is suddenly canceled due to a snowstorm. But it still needs to improve at handling unexpected issues, like a flight attendant who breaks the plane while passengers are boarding for an anticipated on-time departure.

AI also struggles to understand customer intent and infer the reasons behind a customer's request. For example, one airline used AI to automatically rebook my itinerary after my flight was canceled, but routed me to the wrong airport in the same metro area. It didn't understand that changing the airport would create a bigger logistical problem than waiting a short while longer to fly to my original destination. I needed a human gate agent to sort it out and get my trip back on track.

Whether it's a human or AI, poor listening can be costly. The challenge is that those costs are hard to find in your company's finances. But make no mistake, they're there.

The case for good listening

Trader Joe's leads the grocery industry in two important categories.

One is customer service. Trader Joe's is known for friendly, knowledgeable, and helpful employees. The company consistently ranks at or near the top of the American Customer Satisfaction Index.[1]

The second is revenue per square foot.[2] Its stores earn an estimated

$2,171 per square foot. This is more than double the industry average of $964.[3]

One secret to the company's success is a relentless focus on human service. Helpful associates are easy to find in the store's aisles. Human cashiers cheerfully ring up your purchases and get you on your way. Trader Joe's doesn't look at humans as merely an alternative to automation. Those friendly, helpful employees are good at connecting with customers, listening to their needs, and adding extra value to the experience.

Compare that to the shopping experience at the typical grocery store. You can wander the aisles looking for a product and never find an employee who can help. Your two checkout options are a transactional cashier or an automated self-checkout station. This is great if you know exactly what you want, but you don't leave the store feeling any better than when you came in.

Traditional grocery stores use loyalty programs and automated inventory systems to track purchase habits and decide which products sell well and which do not. The drawback of a data-focused approach is that analysts lack context when making decisions about the product assortment to carry in stores. Some products don't sell well because customers don't like them. Others don't sell because customers can't find them; the shelf is empty but the computer thinks it's in stock.

Trader Joe's takes a direct, human approach to understanding its customers and their spending habits. Tara Miller, Trader Joe's Vice President of Marketing, shared on the Trader Joe's podcast that the company doesn't track individual customer data. "Basically, we just don't track our customers," said Miller. "We look at our shelves and we look at what we sell."[4]

This direct approach extends to the Trader Joe's customer service model. "We have live crew members who are smart and fun to talk with," said Miller. "They'll not only help you find what you're looking for and discover new products, they're happy to share their thoughts on these products."

Spending time listening to customers helps Trader Joe's employees sell more products and create a more effective product assortment. It's an example of using humans to add value in ways automation and automatons can't match.

Good listening goes beyond helping you sell more. It also improves efficiency. For one company, good listening cut customer wait times in half.

The customer support team was getting an avalanche of calls. The company made enterprise software, and its customers were confused and upset about a recent update that wasn't intuitive and had several bugs. Customers sometimes had to wait an hour to talk to a person, making them even angrier.

There were a lot of things outside the team's control. They lacked adequate staffing. They weren't responsible for a software design that confused customers, or for releasing an update that didn't work. But one thing the support reps could control was *listening*.

The team was in such a hurry to get through calls that they missed important cues when their customers needed extra help. Customers would hang up thinking their problem was solved only to have to call back a short while later when they discovered another issue related to the first one.

I asked the team to try just one thing: forget about all the customers on hold, impatiently waiting for their turn. Instead, help their current customer fully resolve their issue so they didn't have to call back. Make sure they felt better at the end of the call than they did at the beginning.

It worked. Within days, the average wait time declined by 50 percent. The customer support reps didn't realize how their poor listening was contributing to the call volume. A huge reduction in call volume was a measurable win.

The team's leader decided to take listening to another level. She gathered data on the specific reasons customers were calling, along with sample calls. Then she met with the product team to share the data and listen to calls so the software engineers could hear customers describe their frustrations.

This was a gold mine for the product team since it gave them real data to identify needed fixes and prioritize their work. Those fixes improved the product, eliminated extended wait times, and restored customer confidence to previous levels. It was another quantifiable impact from good listening.

Taking extra time to listen is counterintuitive. It feels inefficient, yet it often results in faster service and happier customers.

A number of years later, I partnered with a company called Balto to test this on a larger scale. Balto makes AI-powered contact center agent support software. We used Balto's AI tools to analyze over 29,000 customer calls. The data revealed some interesting insights about listening.

The AI tools assessed how a customer was feeling at the start of the call and how they felt at the end. The goal was to measure changes in sentiment and discover what agents did to make customers happier or unhappier over the course of a conversation. It worked by identifying and analyzing specific words and phrases that indicated various emotions. Human technicians calibrated the AI software to make sure it was consistent and accurate.

One insight was that asking questions correlated with making customers happier. Agents asked 18.5 questions per call when the customer was happier at the end than they were at the beginning. This was 4.6 questions more than calls where agents made customers unhappy; those calls averaged just 13.9 questions.

You might think it would take longer to ask more questions and make customers happy. The opposite was true. Calls where customers became *un*happy were 25 percent longer on average! When agents made customers happier, the average call length was nearly identical to calls where the customer's mood remained unchanged.[5]

The next insight was even more unexpected. Agents talked more than customers on calls where they made customers happy—60 percent of the time on happy calls compared to just 49 percent of the time on unhappy calls.

It didn't make sense at first. Logically, it seemed that customers would spend more time talking if you ask them more questions. It only started making sense when we listened to the calls or observed employees interacting with customers in person.

Positive customer service interactions follow a consistent pattern of trust and cooperation. The employee creates a human connection with the customer by greeting them and building rapport. They ask the customer questions to learn about their needs as they start to gain the customer's trust. The customer becomes more willing to listen to the employee's suggestions when they feel a personal connection with the employee and sense the employee understands their needs.

Negative customer interactions tend to resemble a tug of war. The customer is wary of the employee's intentions and ability to serve. They don't feel the employee understands their needs or has their best interests at heart, so they question what the employee is asking or doing. The conversation becomes a struggle between the customer and employee, where each person is trying to gain control. That struggle is why interactions take longer when a customer gets upset.

Good listening is more efficient, but being a good human listener requires you to do more than just understand the words a customer is using. You must identify their intent. That's trickier than it might appear.

Listening for intent

There are different levels of listening required to understand a customer's needs.

The first level is understanding what the customer specifically asks for. "I want to pay my bill" literally means the customer wants to pay their bill.

Transactional humans and AI both do generally well with this first level. It's easy for an agent to understand the literal meaning of "pay my bill," especially if this is a routine transaction. An AI voice agent can usually understand that "pay my bill" means the customer wants to make a payment.

The second level of listening is understanding the customer's intent. A customer who says "I want to pay my bill" might just need help completing the transaction. It could also be a signal of a deeper issue. Perhaps the customer received a past due notice and they're concerned about their finances, or they're frustrated because they thought they'd set up automatic payments and can't understand why the payment didn't go through.

AI is getting better at picking up on intent by analyzing multiple pieces of information. Some AI systems can tell if a customer calling to make a payment has received a past due notice. It can tell when the customer has automatic payments enabled on their account and identify that the most recent payment was declined because the credit card on file had expired.

This is an area where transactional humans struggle mightily. They focus on the transaction and miss or ignore additional details that provide a clue to the real issue. Recall the customer service rep for the ticketing app who couldn't fathom that the transfer feature wasn't working. She misunderstood my needs and thought I needed to know how to transfer tickets to my friends. My real need was resolving the error that prevented the transfers from happening.

Humans can succeed at listening where automation and automatons fail. Being attentive makes it easier to understand customer requests. Effective listening skills uncover the intent behind them.

Exercise: Listening skills practice

You probably already know how to listen. These skills come naturally in certain situations, such as when you're talking with a friend who needs your help.

I like to demonstrate this when I'm facilitating customer service training. Participants are asked to find a partner and share a story for 90 seconds. The story can be about anything they wish: a customer service experience, a memorable vacation, or what they had for dinner last night. The content of the story doesn't matter, because we just need to give the listener a story to listen to. At the end of 90 seconds, their partner is asked to take 30 seconds to recap the story they just heard and explain why they feel the story was important to the storyteller.

Participants typically do well with this exercise. They consistently get the main idea of the story and detect its underlying importance. When prompted, participants are able to identify specific techniques they used to enhance their listening. These include facing the storyteller, giving them their full attention, asking clarifying questions, and paraphrasing what they heard to confirm understanding.

This exercise works because it creates two conditions that make it easier for people to be good listeners: intention and focus.

Participants are told ahead of time that they'll be asked to give a recap of the story their partner told and share why they think it's important to the storyteller. Knowing that what they hear will be useful later creates an intention to listen carefully. Giving participants specific things to listen for helps them focus on the story's most important elements.

People participating in the storytelling exercise could easily get distracted by all the other conversations in the room, but most don't. They give their partner full attention, because they know they'll be accountable for detecting the feelings behind what's said.

Try the listening skills exercise with a coworker.

1. One person tells a story for 90 seconds.

2. The other person takes 30 seconds to recap the story and explain its importance.

3. Brainstorm the specific listening techniques used to understand the story.

There's a variation of this exercise that works for written communication. Find samples of customer emails or chat requests. Review them and decide what the customer is likely trying to accomplish. Anticipate those needs and craft a response that fully addresses them. Try to imagine the next logical question your customer would ask, and answer that question, too.

Practice these skills when serving customers. Start every interaction with the intention to discover their needs at both levels: what they're asking for and the intent behind their request. Use the listening skills you already have, like paying attention, asking clarifying questions, and paraphrasing to fully understand your customers' needs.

Let's recap

Being a good listener helps you better understand your customers' needs. This leads to better service and is often more efficient.

Human customer service involves listening to understand a customer's true needs:

1. Identify what your customer is asking for.

2. Understand the intent behind their request.

Try the listening skills exercise to improve your ability to understand your customers. You can practice listening to a coworker, work on your listening skills while serving customers, or practice understanding customers' written needs.

In the next chapter, we'll focus on using empathy to deepen our understanding of customer needs.

CHAPTER 4 NOTES

1 "Supermarkets, Satisfaction Benchmarks by Company," American Customer Satisfaction Index website, accessed January 11, 2026, https://theacsi.org/industries/retail/supermarkets.

2 Trader Joe's financials are not publicly reported, so the sales per square foot figure was derived by consulting multiple online websites, financial analysts, journalists, and other sources for annual revenue and retail square footage estimates.

3 "Food Industry Facts," The Food Industry Association website, accessed January 11, 2026, https://www.fmi.org/our-research/food-industry-facts.

4 "Does Trader Joe's Do Retail Media?" (*Inside Trader Joe's Podcast*, March 24, 2025).

5 You can read more about the author's research on the sentiment arc here: https://www.toistersolutions.com/blog/sentiment-arc.

CHAPTER FIVE

Empathy

I HAD LESS THAN 30 MINUTES, and I was starting to freak out.

A client had hired me to facilitate a remote training session with her team. She rearranged work schedules and added extra coverage so everyone could attend. For the past few weeks, she'd been hyping up the session to get the team excited.

Now, just before the webinar was about to start, I couldn't get the webinar software to work. I dreaded letting my client down. She'd worked so hard to organize this training session!

I frantically searched for a technical support number. "This is the last straw," I thought to myself, navigating through the phone menu and waiting on hold. The webinar software had been getting increasingly difficult to use. It worked okay for attendees, but there were problems on the back end. There were many times I'd had to find a workaround to keep it running. I resolved to find a different webinar provider once I got through this session.

Miraculously, I was quickly connected with a support agent. A real human! She was calm, capable, and empathetic. The agent expertly walked me through a troubleshooting process and got the software working with just a few minutes to spare before my client's employees began logging into the webinar. I started feeling relieved that I wasn't going to let my client down after all.

That's when the agent did something completely unexpected. "I know your webinar is about to start," she said. "While I'm confident we solved the issue, I'm going to stay on the line while you begin. I'll be right here to help in case you need me. If everything goes smoothly, and I think it will, I'll quietly get off the line and you can run your meeting."

Her confidence and support made me feel a million times better. My anxiety disappeared, buoyed by the reassurance that she was waiting to help if needed. I was able to focus my energy on running a great webinar for my client. The agent was right that the software was working perfectly, and my webinar went off without a hitch.

The support agent didn't just solve the issue. She empathized with the nervousness I felt about the webinar software not working at a critical time. The agent added extra human value by providing reassurance that she'd be there if needed. Her supportive approach helped me shift my focus back to where it belonged—serving my client.

Her actions that day convinced me to postpone my planned cancellation of the webinar service. The software still wasn't great, but I felt better knowing the kind of human support that was available if something went wrong. I ultimately kept my subscription for two more years before finally switching to a better product.

It's refreshing to encounter a support agent like that—someone who will stay on the phone to walk you back from your panic and verify that everything is working. She was the kind of agent whose service transcends product limitations and convinces you to remain a customer.

In this chapter, we'll explore how empathy is a uniquely human skill that can help the people you serve feel better. I'll share specific techniques you can use to develop your empathy superpowers. But first, let's look at the impact on customers when we *don't* empathize.

Automatons are cold

It was a cold winter, and Larry was running low on propane to heat his home.

People in rural areas often rely on propane in the winter. There are no gas lines feeding the property like there are in the city. Propane is used the same way people in the city use natural gas: heating the home, cooking, and so on. The propane is delivered via truck and pumped into an onsite storage tank.

The propane company had missed a scheduled delivery to Larry's home. It was human error; those things sometimes happen. Rescheduling the delivery wouldn't be a big deal if Larry's tank hadn't already been dangerously low on fuel.

The customer service rep didn't perceive Larry's sense of urgency. They assumed the issue was just a matter of rescheduling a missed delivery. A lack of empathy caused the rep to miss clear signals that Larry was worried.

The cold winter meant Larry was burning more propane than usual. Running out of propane wasn't Larry's true worry. His true worry was not being able to heat his home.

The tank got down to two percent, but nobody at the propane company could understand the urgency. The company had automation that suggested the tank was fuller and automatons who only focused on propane delivery schedules. There were no humans who would expedite a resolution.

Larry's propane tank ran out.

Fortunately, Larry was able to contact another company that could start service right away and fill his tank. He wasn't without propane for very long, but that lack of empathy cost the original company a long-time customer.

The *Merriam-Webster* dictionary defines empathy this way: "the action of understanding, being aware of, being sensitive to, and vicariously experiencing the feelings, thoughts, and experience of another."[1] In customer service, empathizing means understanding the emotions your customer is experiencing and taking action to help them feel better.

The webinar software support rep provided a wonderful example of empathy. She heard me say that I was about to facilitate a webinar for a client and understood that I was nervous about the software not working when my client was counting on me. Staying on the line to be sure things went smoothly restored my confidence that everything would be okay and allowed me to focus on doing a great job for my client.

The type of service I received from the webinar support rep is rare. Customer service has an empathy problem. Too many employees miss their customers' emotional cues or don't know what to do with them.

It's no wonder customers often prefer self-service. It can feel faster and easier than dealing with an automaton. A study by Gartner found that 51 percent of customers seek help on third-party sites like Google, YouTube, and Reddit before contacting a company for support.[2]

Technical support employees follow a tightly-scripted trouble-shooting routine in which empathy and personality aren't included. Customer service reps are judged by how closely they follow the script and how quickly they close each support ticket, without regard to how the customer feels about the experience. One agent tearfully confessed, "They give me just six minutes to fix each customer's issue. I don't have time to make them feel better."

Some employees really don't care. They steamroll past customer feelings because empathy isn't even on their radar. Or maybe they once cared, but have become so fatigued that they've stopped trying.

A power surge knocked out the power to my neighborhood, resulting in thousands of dollars in damage to many homes, including mine. The surge was caused by the electric company's faulty equipment, but the company was unresponsive and unhelpful. It took nearly three days and multiple calls to get power restored so I could assess the damage. Most of my attempts to call were thwarted by an annoying voice agent that constantly repeated, "That's not what I expected!" when I asked for a human; a live agent; a real person; someone who cares; someone who gives a damn; someone who has the power to restore my power; or when I simply kept saying "help."

When I finally reached an employee, he acted like talking to me was the biggest inconvenience imaginable. He was rude. I could hear him sigh as he tapped away at his keyboard. Not once did he say he was sorry I had been without power, or that his company's negligence had wrought chaos on my neighborhood, or that the company relied so much on automation that it failed miserably at being human.

I could sort of empathize with the customer service employee. His company had caused a huge problem. Maybe he was told to be a jerk because the utility knew it faced a big liability for the damage it caused. Perhaps he resented taking call after call from anxious, angry customers who'd been trying to get help for days. But whatever the cause, treating customers inhumanely and without empathy only made a bad situation worse.

Empathy isn't just a skill you use for solving problems. It can help you find better ways to serve your customers. Failing to empathize is a missed opportunity.

An employee in a store that provides shipping services helped a customer put together a package for shipment. The customer didn't have a box, so the employee indicated the store sold boxes of various sizes and showed the customer where they were located.

There was nothing inherently wrong with the transaction, but the employee completely missed several cues that would have made the experience better. The customer was really worried about making sure the package's fragile contents made it safely to their destination. The customer left the store happy to check a chore off their to-do list, but uneasy about what would happen to their shipment.

Another employee handled a similar transaction very differently. She sensed the customer's concern and asked if the contents were fragile. When the customer said they were, she suggested the customer allow her to pack the shipment for them. It would cost a little extra, she explained, but the fragile contents would be expertly protected and her packing service included extra insurance in case anything broke. You could see the relief on the customer's face as they realized the employee truly understood their needs and would take care to make sure the shipment arrived safely.

Two employees in the same store took very different approaches. One looked at the customer as a transaction, and that customer left feeling uneasy. The other sensed the customer's anxiety, asked questions to understand it, and provided a better solution that left the customer feeling confident.

In my experience, employees generally enjoy using empathy skills to help customers. You probably want to help your customers, too. That's why you got into the customer service business. It's why you're reading this book.

Empathy is one place where AI can help or hinder.

AI's role in customer empathy

Good help was hard to find in the old days of video rental stores.

They were staffed with employees whose greatest joy was assessing late fees. Employees couldn't be bothered to suggest a movie that fit your mood and tastes, or suggest a hidden gem. The best you could hope for was to search through racks that were nominally organized by genre—comedies, action flicks, dramas, new releases, and so on.

Non-chain stores tended to have more helpful employees. Some were video savants who could size you up with a few questions and make a spot-on recommendation. You considered yourself lucky if you had a store in your neighborhood with employees like that.

Netflix changed the video rental customer service game with its AI-powered recommendation software. It analyzed your viewing history and the ratings you gave to the various movies and shows you watched. The software compared your ratings to how other viewers rated the same movies and shows and used that data to predict additional movies and shows you might like. Its ability to process massive amounts of data made it significantly more useful than the disaffected automaton-clerk at the rental store.

Napoleon Dynamite threw a wrench into the algorithm. The 2004 indie cult classic was a polarizing film. People either loved or hated its off-beat humor and quirky characters. There wasn't a lot of middle ground. The AI software struggled to predict whether people would like it, because the movie was so different from everything else.

That polarization created a problem for Netflix. In 2007, one analyst found that the system could predict how a viewer would rate the average movie on a one-to-five star scale within eight-tenths of a star. The system's predictions for how viewers would rate *Napoleon Dynamite* were off by 1.2 stars on average.[3]

Part of the challenge was that the software was too rational. When someone gave films similar ratings, it looked at what movies had in common. If you gave high marks to screwball 80's high school comedies, and you gave *Weird Science* a higher rating than *Sixteen Candles*, the algorithm might suggest *Teen Wolf* for your next watch.

At first glance, *Napoleon Dynamite* seemed like it would fit that profile. The visual aesthetic feels like the movie is set in the 80's, even though it's set in 2004. The film is quirky rather than screwball. It's so quirky that people find it hard to explain why it's so funny.

AI missed the human side of the equation. Being a fan of that movie is a shared human experience. You talk to your friends about it. You share opinions, quote favorite lines, and relive your favorite scenes. You feel a need to compliment a stranger wearing a Rex Kwon Do t-shirt because it's a reference to a funny scene from the movie.

Some of you reading this will wonder why I didn't mention the more ubiquitous "Vote for Pedro" t-shirt, and that insider knowledge is part of the shared experience as well.

AI is great for rational analysis, but detecting and responding appropriately to human feelings is a whole different ballgame. As one person told me, "I don't mind AI telling me I'm due to visit my doctor for a routine check-up, but I don't want it telling me I have cancer."

That's why getting poor service from AI results in such a bad feeling. It's infuriating when a bot or AI voice agent can't or won't help you and refuses to route you to a human. The software has no sense of the frustration it's causing or how badly it's missing the mark. It just keeps trying.

One place where AI actually shines is giving human employees more capacity for empathy. AI is able to handle a lot of simple transactions that used to require a human. This allows employees to spend more time on the hard stuff that requires human skills such as empathy.

Love's Travel Stops provides a great example. One of the services Love's provides is emergency roadside assistance for commercial trucks. A truck driver can call the hotline to request a mechanic if their truck breaks down.

Staffing used to be a big challenge. It was hard to have enough agents available to answer more than 30,000 calls per month. The wait time to speak to an agent averaged nine minutes, which can feel like an eternity when time is money for a stranded driver. Love's was able to use an AI voice agent to answer calls and reduce the average wait time to just 9 seconds.[4]

They partnered with a company called Replicant to install the AI voice agent. The AI agent handles routine requests, such as dispatching a mechanic to a stranded driver. Most drivers are fine using the AI agent for simple roadside assistance since it's fast, simple, and they're able to get help right away. Answering the phone quickly and offering immediate assistance reduced abandoned phone calls by 85 percent. Meanwhile, human agents are available for more complex needs, or for nervous drivers who just prefer to speak to a person.

Brien Mikell, Director of Contact Center Operations, explained that agents enjoyed this shift from primarily transactional calls to calls requiring them to listen to drivers' unique needs, empathize with them, and find ways to help them get back on the road. Giving agents more interesting work helped reduce attrition by 50 percent, so staffing was no longer a big problem.

Empathy is easy and even fun when employees believe they can use it to make a difference. It's amazingly empowering to help a customer feel a sense of relief and know that you contributed to them having a better experience.

Empathizing with humans

Missing a flight is stressful.

Just the thought of it is scary. I've seen panicked customers racing through the airport to make a connecting flight. I missed a flight myself while writing this chapter because my first flight encountered multiple delays, so I know exactly how it feels. You worry about the disruption to your travel plans, the inconvenience of finding another flight option, and whether you'll have to pay more to be re-accommodated.

I once witnessed an airline passenger miss her flight because she was too busy drinking at the bar. The airport bar was about 50 feet from her gate, but she still managed to miss the clearly-audible boarding announcements. It was too late when she finally noticed the time and frantically staggered to the gate for her already-departed flight.

The angry passenger blamed the airline gate agent for her missed flight. He didn't want to listen to her drunken rant and quickly dismissed her concerns in a misguided attempt to get her to accept responsibility and go away. This made the passenger even more furious, and she began yelling.

A second airline employee approached. He used empathy to recognize the real issue: the passenger was embarrassed that she'd missed the flight and nervous about the consequences. The alcohol made her heightened emotions difficult to control.

He stood next to the passenger so he was literally on her side, rather than standing in front of her. "You shouldn't have to feel this way," he said. "Tell me what happened."

The passenger's demeanor immediately changed. She saw the employee wanted to help, not argue. He listened intently and without judgment as she described missing her flight and the poor treatment she felt she received from the first gate agent.

The employee's empathetic listening defused the situation. It became boring enough that other passengers in the terminal stopped paying attention. People put away their phones when they realized there wasn't going to be any viral content to capture on video.

The employee made sure the passenger was feeling better and then deftly moved the conversation toward a solution. He knew she needed some time to sober up, and then he could get her on another flight. The employee avoided mentioning the first part and focused instead on helping the passenger get rebooked on a later flight that would give her time to recover.

The airline employee demonstrated a master class in empathy. These skills aren't only effective with drunken customers, as they work with nearly any human who needs your help. Let's break it down.

Empathy techniques

Empathy comes easily if you've shared the same experience as your customer.

The airline employee would know exactly how to help the drunken passenger feel better if he had also missed a flight while getting intoxicated in an airport bar. That probably hadn't happened, so he'd need to find a different, but relatable, experience to draw upon.

Three questions can help.

Imagine you're the airline employee. Let's go through the three questions together and see if we can find a way to empathize with the drunken passenger who missed her flight.

Question 1: Why was the customer upset? She was upset because she missed her flight, which disrupted her travel plans. She was probably embarrassed because she knew deep down that missing the flight was her fault. The alcohol made it difficult for her to regulate her emotions. Embarrassment can quickly turn to anger when a customer makes a mistake.

Question 2: Have you ever had a similar experience? You probably know exactly how the passenger felt if you've ever gotten drunk and done something dumb. Even if you don't drink, you've probably made an embarrassing mistake that you wished was somebody else's fault. For example, I once booked a flight for the wrong day and arrived at the airport to discover I didn't have a seat on the flight! It was tempting to blame the airline for the mixup, but the error was my fault. I worried about the disruption to my travel plans and was embarrassed about making the mistake—exactly the same emotions the drunken passenger experienced.

Question 3: What would have made you feel better? I'll never forget the airline employee who helped me. He was patient, understanding, and kind. He saved me from further embarrassment by assuring me it was a common error, and he was happy to help me fix it. The employee found me a seat on a flight that day and waived the change fee because he knew it was an honest mistake. It was a huge relief.

That same approach worked wonders with the drunken passenger. The second airline employee avoided blaming her and causing further embarrassment. He made it clear he was on her side and that he wanted to help. Her anger subsided and then turned to relief when he was able to assist her.

Understanding how a customer feels is the first step. The next step is using that knowledge to help the customer feel better. You can use the LAURA technique to put empathy into action:

1. L = Listen
2. A = Acknowledge
3. U = Understand
4. R = Relate
5. A = Act

The airline gate agent applied the LAURA technique with the drunken passenger. He started by listening to the passenger ranting to his co-worker. The gate agent intervened and acknowledged her feelings by saying, "You shouldn't have to feel this way." Then he sought to better understand the situation by inviting her to share more. He related to her emotions as she told her story and understood that she was anxious about having missed her flight and embarrassed about why she didn't make it to the gate in time. Finally, the agent took action by helping the passenger get booked on a later flight.

It can be difficult to remember the five steps in the LAURA technique until you've practiced it a bit. A shortcut is to imagine an unflappable customer service rep named Laura who is kind, caring, and empathetic. Just try to be like Laura when you're serving an upset customer and you'll often find a way to empathize naturally.

Let's recap

Empathy is the process of being able to understand how another person is feeling.

Use empathy to identify and address your customer's emotional needs. This happens naturally if you've been in the same situation that your customer is experiencing. If you've not been there before, use three questions to find a relatable experience:

1. Why is the customer upset?
2. Have you ever had a similar experience?
3. What would have made you feel better?

The LAURA technique can help you empathize with customers and make them feel better:

1. L = Listen
2. A = Acknowledge
3. U = Understand
4. R = Relate
5. A = Act

The next chapter will move us to advocacy, the third set of human service skills. We'll start with proactive service.

CHAPTER 5 NOTES

1   *Merriam-Webster.com*, "empathy (n.)," accessed January 11, 2026, https://www.merriam-webster.com/dictionary/empathy.

2   "Gartner Survey Finds More Than Half of Customer Service Journeys Now Start on Third-Party Platforms," Gartner press release, July 23, 2025, https://www.gartner.com/en/newsroom/press-releases/2025-07-23-gartner-survey-finds-more-than-half-of-customer-service-journeys-now-start-on-third-party-platforms.

3   Clive Thompson, "If You Liked This, You're Sure to Love That," (*The New York Times Magazine*, November 21, 2008), https://www.nytimes.com/2008/11/23/magazine/23Netflix-t.html.

4   "From roadblocks to rapid response: how Love's saved money and cut wait times with Replicant," Replicant website, accessed January 11, 2026, https://www.replicant.com/case-studies/loves.

5   "Love's Travel Stops: AI and the Art of Next-gen Service," (Replicant, *Dialed In Podcast*, Episode 17), accessed January 11, 2026, https://www.youtube.com/watch?v=C66PloEULOs&t=700s.

SECTION THREE:
Advocacy

Proactive

PARKING WAS PREDOMINANTLY A CASH BUSINESS IN 2005.

That year, the Portland International Airport, called PDX for short, implemented self-service payment technology. The goal was to improve efficiency and reduce operating costs as the airport expanded.

That same technology was already in use at other airports in the United States, but adoption rates were low. The average airport got just 40 percent of its customers to pay for parking using self-service. Most people still preferred waiting in line for a cashier.

PDX set its sights higher. It set a goal to double the national average and get 80 percent of parkers to use self-service. To accomplish this, the airport made sure self-service kiosks were readily available at access points throughout the garage so customers didn't have to go out of their way to make a payment. Exit gates were equipped with credit card readers so customers could bypass the kiosks and pay for parking at the exit.

Technology alone wasn't enough to encourage customers to use self-service to pay for parking. Many were skeptical of the self-service machines. Others thought driving up to a cashier as they always did would be easier. Quite a few paid at the cashier booth out of habit. They all needed a nudge if they were going to change their behavior.

I was the training director for the company that managed the airport parking. It was my job to help our local team achieve the 80 percent self-service adoption goal. Proactive human service was central to our strategy.

The self-service technology meant fewer cashiers would be needed. We retrained them to become parking ambassadors. Their new role was to help customers discover that using the self-service machines to pay for parking was faster and easier than driving up to a cashier booth. They were asked to stand in front of the self-service kiosks and invite parkers to give the machines a try, and then guide customers through the process if they wanted extra help.

This was a big mindset shift for the cashiers. Their job used to be re-active. They used to wait for a car to pull up to their booth. The driver would hand them a parking ticket and they'd ring up the transaction. Now cashiers were asked to be proactive.

Cashiers went through an initial training program to learn how to be a parking ambassador. There were three basic steps. The first was to greet every customer who walked into their area using the 10 and 5 technique to capture the customer's attention. (Chapter Two describes the 10 and 5 technique.) The second was to invite customers to try using a self-service kiosk. The third was to offer guidance to customers who wanted it, but, crucially, they were to let customers do the transaction themselves so people would discover how easy it was to use the machines.

I worked with the team to refine our approach. Employees exper-imented with different ways to capture a customer's attention and entice them to use the machine. They gave feedback on what worked and what didn't. Supervisors worked alongside the ambassadors to help document and share best practices.

Nearly every employee embraced their new role. They enjoyed the opportunity to proactively offer assistance and were pleasantly surprised at the overwhelmingly positive reaction from customers. Employees also enjoyed giving their input to help shape best practices.

The team knew the ambassador role wouldn't last forever. Someday, the public would feel more comfortable using self-service and the am-bassadors would no longer be necessary. The better the ambassadors did their new job, the sooner that day would come.

Losing jobs is a common concern when automation enters the

picture. Fortunately, the parking operation was growing, so those employees would be needed in other roles. The overall staff size would grow during the first year of the project, and then shrink slightly through normal attrition. It helped morale that employees knew they weren't going to lose their jobs to a kiosk.

The ambassador program was a success. The payment kiosk adoption rate reached 80 percent just eight months after launching the self-service technology. Proactive customer service helped double the national average in less than a year.

Proactive service helps customers have a better experience by addressing unrealized needs. It could be offering directions to someone who looks lost, holding a door for someone with their arms full of packages, or giving a customer an insider tip on how to get the most out of a new purchase. At PDX, proactive service meant helping parkers save time and effort by showing them how to use the self-service kiosk. Most customers were delighted when they realized how easy it was.

In this chapter, we'll explore the problems caused by strictly reactive service, discuss how proactive service can improve customer experience, highlight the business case for being proactive, and identify proactive human customer service techniques.

When help is *not* on the way

Customers get frustrated when employees aren't available to help.

I once encountered an elderly woman standing in front of a self-service kiosk in a parking garage outside a medical clinic. She was clearly confused about how to pay for parking and leave the garage. She looked at me as I approached with an expression that suggested she could use some help. It's the kind of expression we humans easily recognize.

Her confusion brought me back to the PDX project I'd worked on 20 years earlier. The current process of paying for parking is similar to what it was back then, and I was happy to help this fellow parker figure out how to pay and exit the garage.

The screen on the self-service kiosk indicated she'd already paid for her parking. I reassured her that she had completed the first step and then walked her through the process for driving up to the exit and scanning her ticket to open the gate so she could leave the garage. "Make sure you keep your ticket handy so you can scan it at the gate," I reminded her before using the kiosk to pay my own parking fee.

The elderly woman was two cars in front of me when I got my car in line at the garage exit. I could see the ticket in her hand, arm flailing around while she tried to find the right place to scan her ticket. She finally aligned the barcode on her ticket with the reader on the machine and the exit gate opened.

Unfortunately, she took so long to get resettled in her car that the exit gate closed before she could pull forward and leave the garage. The ticket she had scanned was now canceled since the system was programmed to allow just one exit per ticket. Try as she might, she couldn't get the gate to open again.

A pedestrian walking by saw what happened and offered assistance. He went to the driver's-side window and talked to the woman as they both tried to figure out how to call someone for help. There wasn't an obvious way to contact the medical clinic or a garage employee. More cars started lining up at the single exit gate while the two searched for a way to get assistance.

The driver in front of me got out of his car to help. He had figured out the garage's ticket-based entry and exit system and quickly devised a plan. He flagged down a driver about to enter the garage in the adjacent lane, explained the situation, and enlisted that driver's help to execute a clever work-around.

The entering driver pulled a ticket. The entrance gate opened, but the driver didn't drive forward. He waited until the gate closed so the parking system now registered that ticket as belonging to someone who had driven into the garage.

The garage had a short grace period before customers were charged for parking. This meant the ticket could be used to exit the garage without payment if it was used quickly.

The driver whose car was in front of mine took the ticket from the driver at the entrance and walked over to the exit lane where he used the ticket to open the gate. The elderly driver was ready this time and drove out. Then the driver in the entrance lane pulled a new ticket and entered the garage normally.

Three different people proactively offered to help the woman figure out the parking garage automation. None were employees. We all saw someone who needed help and did the human thing.

Customer service is not always easy to get when you need it. Automated parking garages aren't staffed to help the occasional flummoxed driver. Drug store customers must summon an employee to unlock deodorant. Finding a department store employee to help you is about as likely as finding Bigfoot. Call customer service with an urgent issue, and be prepared to wait on hold for an eternity to speak to a live agent.

Hunting for help is frustrating and annoying to customers. Many decide to take their business somewhere else when help is not readily available.

There are other times when a customer could use extra help, but might not realize it yet. Failing to anticipate and address unrealized customer needs is a missed opportunity. Worse, it's the start of a service failure.

For example, neatly packaging a fast food order without adding napkins to the bag will disappoint a customer when they need to wipe their hands. The customer didn't explicitly ask for napkins, but they're still likely to have a negative feeling about their experience with the restaurant as they wipe burger juice on their pants.

Customers often share information that can be used to proactively help the next customer, but that feedback is frequently ignored. One cable company has a policy that five customers from the same service area must complain about a service interruption before it's flagged as an outage and a technician can be dispatched to look into it. Meanwhile, many more customers are affected by losing their cable and internet service.

Employees at companies like that aren't empowered to listen to customers who report problems. Many privately tell me they don't have any means to share customer feedback, so it never gets shared. The same problems just keep happening.

I once placed an order at a fast food counter and noticed that the customer-facing register screen was broken. It was supposed to show my order and total amount due, but instead the screen mirrored the cashier's view of the register. I could see all of the menu buttons and functions as if I were the cashier about to ring up my own purchase.

When I pointed it out to the cashier, she shrugged and told me it had been broken for a while. Another employee chimed in and said, "It's been like that since I started working here, and that's been two years." It's hard for employees to be proactive when they can't even get broken equipment fixed.

Some service needs are predictable based on historical data, but that data needs to be analyzed and acted upon. For instance, an airport operations team knows the restrooms will need cleaning at certain intervals throughout the day because of regular flight schedules. Top-rated airports proactively schedule cleaning around these known patterns. They also monitor the restrooms throughout the day in case they need extra attention.

Not every airport does this. Some airports ignore predictable service patterns and fail to clean restrooms when it's needed. And on more than one occasion, I've watched an employee walk into an airport restroom, initial the check sheet on the wall to indicate they've attended to the restroom, and walk right out without lifting a finger to clean it. Proactive service won't happen if employees don't take pride in their work.

Proactive customer service can be difficult. Someone has to be paying attention, recognize a customer need, and be ready to meet it. Technology is making that easier to do.

AI can make service more proactive

One place where AI shines is in helping companies provide more proactive customer service.

A cable company technician told me the AI troubleshooting tools he uses can identify network issues and diagnose root causes faster than ever before. This helps the company proactively notify customers about a problem and provide an accurate estimated time to repair it. Sending proactive notices minimizes the number of customers who contact the company to report the problem.

A caseworker who helps patients with disease management uses AI to prioritize her daily patient outreach. Her software analyzes a complicated array of factors from well over a hundred assigned patients to help her anticipate patient needs and decide who to contact each day. Using AI allows her to spend more time connecting with patients and less time managing her schedule.

Contact centers are now using AI-powered software to analyze voice and text conversations in real time. This data can identify a spike in contacts about a particular issue so it can be addressed more quickly. It can also alert a supervisor to an agent who's struggling and needs coaching before too many customers are affected.

AI can help make customer service more proactive, but it's not infallible. There are times when human service still adds value. For instance, ride-share apps use AI to give passengers real-time arrival updates when a driver is on the way. Those updates can be wildly inaccurate if unexpected congestion appears. A direct contact from the human driver is more helpful to the customer than the inaccurate updates in the app when that happens.

Proactive human service

Moving into a senior living community is a tough decision.

The inevitability of aging can be hard to accept. Maintaining a home gets more difficult as you lose the strength, mobility, and balance to do many of the daily chores you once took for granted. Yet leaving that home feels like losing independence and familiarity.

Many prospective residents struggle with the choice to leave behind a home they've lived in for decades. They must often part with a lifetime of personal possessions that won't fit in their new, smaller home. A cherished garden or a dream kitchen are now in the rear view mirror.

Finances complicate the decision. Senior living communities can be expensive. Many residents must sell their homes to afford the costly entry fee. And unlike owning a home, that entry fee doesn't appreciate in value.

Losing a spouse or partner hastens the decision for some people. It can also make it more difficult to make the choice when your trusted confidant and lifetime companion is no longer there to discuss it with you. Change is difficult.

Human connection can be the deciding factor. Senior living residents have access to a whole community of potential friends. The loneliness of living alone is replaced with an abundant social life. Caring employees are there to look out for residents' physical and emotional well-being.

Lifespace Communities owns and manages senior living communities. The company succeeds by prioritizing human connection. One way they do this is through proactive service. Their communities have multiple proactive procedures to ensure residents feel a sense of belonging.

Prospective residents have a chance to meet people with similar interests when they visit. It helps them discover the activities the community offers and see how easily they'll be able to make new friends. It also gives them a chance to ask residents about their experience moving from their home into the community.

The dining room is another place where employees proactively foster a sense of belonging. There's often a designated "friendship table" in the dining room where new residents can meet others. Dining room employees look for signs of connection among residents and encourage people to sit at tables where employees know they're likely to create connections with other residents.

Housekeepers proactively keep an eye out for signs of connection or disconnection when they clean residents' apartments. A resident who rarely leaves and keeps their curtains drawn might be feeling lonely and disengaged. Housekeepers are encouraged to have a cup of coffee with the resident just to chat for a bit before resuming their cleaning tasks.

Nikki Kresse, Lifespace's Chief People and Experience Officer, told me that these examples of proactive service are an intentional part of the resident experience. "Our North Star emotion is a desire to belong," explained Kresse. Looking out for unrealized resident needs helps employees proactively identify and act upon opportunities to help create that sense of belonging.

Being human while serving customers isn't something you can take for granted. At Lifespace, employees are hired for their natural inclination towards human service. "If they aren't caring at their core, it's hard to train someone to do that," said Kresse.

Proactive service requires employees to do two things. First, you have to be observant so you can identify customer needs even before the customer realizes it. Second, you have to be ready and willing to address those needs.

Transactional employees struggle with awareness. I once arrived in my designated room for a presentation only to discover that some of the tables and chairs had been set up behind a giant pillar blocking the view of the front of the room. The automatons who'd set up the room followed the room setup procedure precisely: the correct number of tables and chairs were lined up in the correct formation. But they missed the big obvious pillar because they weren't on the lookout for additional or unrealized needs.

I walk the room before every presentation so I can identify issues. Sitting in different parts of the room helps me see my presentation the way my audience will see it. It helps me make adjustments so I can ensure everyone has a good view. The giant pillar was impossible to overlook.

The second part of proactive customer service, being ready and willing to address unmet needs, is often the easier of the two steps. There was an empty space in the room where the table and chairs could be moved so people sitting there could see.

Proactive service can also help prevent a small issue from becoming a big one. One of my favorite techniques for doing this is called the preemptive acknowledgment. It works by identifying an issue and acknowledging it before your customer has a chance to get upset.

There's a good chance someone's used this technique on you, and it probably worked. Think about a time when you went to a restaurant on a busy evening. You place your order and then settle into a nice conversation with your dining companions. Time goes by, and you realize your order is taking longer than it should. People who were seated after you have already gotten their meals. You start to feel the first signs of frustration.

Just then, your server appears. "Thank you for being so patient," they say. "I checked with the kitchen and your order will be right out. In the meantime, can I refill your drinks?" Your meal arrives soon after and it's fantastic.

What could have become a poor experience is now a non-issue because your server acknowledged the frustration and took action to solve it before you got upset or had to ask for an update.

The preemptive acknowledgment works in a wide variety of situations. It's especially helpful when something is going to be late, an error has been made, or a product or service is going to be different than expected.

When I managed a contact center, my team proactively tracked all orders where a customer upgraded to express shipping. Those orders were sometimes late, which would be an unpleasant surprise to a customer who paid extra to have it delivered faster. Knowing the order would be late before it actually became late allowed the team to use preemptive acknowledgment. They would contact customers with the bad news and offer a solution, if possible, or an apology and a refund of the express shipping costs if nothing else could be done. Customers were generally understanding, and far fewer got upset compared to customers who didn't get a proactive notice that their order wasn't arriving as expected.

That was a long time ago, when tracking packages was a very manual process. Most of that is automated now, with software able to monitor shipments and automatically notify customers of changes to a planned delivery.

Automated messages are fine for little things like a sweater or a pair of shoes. But proactive human service adds value for bigger ticket items like a furniture delivery that's running behind schedule. Customers appreciate hearing from someone able to share information about the delay and provide options to make it less inconvenient.

Proactive human service is value-added

There's a strong business case for proactive human service.

Making more humans available to help customers seems inefficient at first glance. It cost the airport money to have human ambassadors stationed in front of the parking kiosks at PDX. Asking housekeepers to have a cup of coffee with a resident who seems lonely means that housekeeper gets less cleaning done that day. Your CFO is starting to get uncomfortable just thinking about the extra expense.

The payoff comes when you look at the big picture. PDX took just eight months to double the average self-service usage rate compared to similar airports using the same self-service parking equipment. Employees were eventually transitioned into other roles once the public became accustomed to using the self-service machines. The parking operation was able to expand and serve more customers without adding staff.

Lifespace attracts more residents and keeps them happy by asking employees to prioritize resident wellbeing over tasks. Those residents encourage their friends to join them and move into their Lifespace community, which is powerful word-of-mouth advertising.

Top-performing retail stores know the value of having enough staff to provide proactive customer service. Employees stationed on the sales floor help customers make more purchases by offering assistance and suggestive selling. Their presence also reduces shoplifting.

Macy's, a department store chain more known for cost-cutting in recent years, ran an experiment by adding additional staff to the handbag and women's shoe departments. Revenue increased by six percent by having more employees available to proactively greet and assist customers.[1]

I once ran an experiment with a group of contact center agents who helped customers place orders. Agents were asked to focus on the needs of each individual customer and adapt their approach to the cues they observed. They efficiently moved through the call when it was clear the customer knew exactly what they wanted, avoiding wasting time with upsells or other offers. They proactively offered more assistance when they detected a customer was open to browsing or needed extra advice.

Proactively adjusting their approach to each individual customer paid off. The agents were able to bring in more revenue per shift when they identified each customer's needs. As an added benefit, their calls were also shorter on average.

A parking enforcement team on a college campus saved the equivalent of two full-time employees by focusing on proactive customer service. One of the team's responsibilities was writing parking tickets for vehicles parked in the wrong place or people who hadn't paid the correct parking fee. The administration frequently waived the ticket fees on appeal because its primary goal was ensuring people could access the campus, not collecting fees from faculty, staff, and students. Handling appeals was a time-consuming process for parking employees.

The enforcement manager asked his team to focus on catching people before they parked in the wrong place or paid an incorrect fee. The goal was to offer proactive assistance about where they could park or share information about the appropriate parking fee. Faculty, staff, and students were happier about receiving fewer tickets, and the parking department was able to redeploy employees to other tasks since they were spending less time handling appeals.

Building your proactive human service skills takes some practice. If you're ready, let's try it out.

Proactive human service techniques

It's easier to offer proactive human service when you adopt an "extra mile" mindset.

Going the extra mile means giving an effort that exceeds a customer's expectations. It's unrealistic to do this with every interaction. Sometimes, a cup of coffee is just a cup of coffee. Other times, a customer appreciates a quick chat or some extra assistance.

Employees with an extra-mile mindset are alert to opportunities to proactively do something more for a customer. They listen and observe customer cues to spot an unrealized need, and then spring into action.

Try practicing this mindset for a day. Be alert for cues that a customer could use extra help. Do your best to anticipate a need before your customer realizes they need it.

Here are a few examples from this chapter:

- Parking ambassadors invited customers to save time by using self-service.
- Housekeepers had a cup of coffee with residents when they needed companionship.
- Strangers helped a confused customer escape a parking garage.

The next step is taking action when you spot an opportunity, drawing on personal experience to know what to do.

You can also use your powers of observation to prevent customer anger. Practice using the preemptive acknowledgment technique with your customers.

1. Identify an issue before your customer gets upset.
2. Acknowledge the issue and offer a solution.

Research shows that thanking the customer can be more powerful than apologizing for small issues like a short delay.[2] Saying, "Thank you for waiting" or "I really appreciate your patience" can make customers feel better than if you said, "I'm sorry about the wait." Try adding a thank you when you apply the preemptive acknowledgment technique.

Let's recap

Proactive service helps customers have a better experience by addressing an unrealized need.

There are two steps to providing proactive human service:

1. Look for unrealized customer needs.
2. Take action when you see them.

You can also use the principles of proactive service to minimize the impact of service failures by applying the preemptive acknowledgment technique. Identifying and acknowledging a problem before your customer gets upset can make a small issue feel like a non-event.

In the next chapter, we'll turn our attention to providing solutions to problems that require human intervention.

CHAPTER 6 NOTES

1 Motley Fool Transcribing, "Macy's (M) Q3 2024 Earnings Call Transcript," (*The Motley Fool*, December 12, 2024), https://www.fool.com/earnings/call-transcripts/2024/12/12/macys-m-q3-2024-earnings-call-transcript.

2 Yanfen You, Xiaojing Yang, and Xiaoyan Deng, "When and Why Saying 'Thank You' Is Better Than Saying 'Sorry' in Redressing Service Failures: The Role of Self-Esteem," (*Journal of Marketing*, 84(2), 133-150, December 17, 2019), https://doi.org/10.1177/0022242919889894.

CHAPTER SEVEN
Solving Problems

A CUSTOMER CALLED WITH AN URGENT ORDER.

Donna took the call. She checked inventory for the item her customer wanted. It was out of stock and couldn't be shipped by the time the customer needed it.

Backorders are usually routine. You have options if a sweater you had your eye on is out of stock: you can decide to wait until it's back in stock, you might be willing to purchase a different sweater from the same company or somewhere else, or you can choose to skip the purchase completely.

That's what a customer would normally do, but not this customer. Donna's customer was a hospital. The item the hospital needed was a heart stent—a particular model in a particular size for a patient scheduled for a potentially lifesaving procedure the next day.

Donna recognized the urgency. She knew normal processes and procedures didn't apply. If there was a solution to be found, she had to find it.

She started with the warehouse. Inventory was usually accurate, but not always. Perhaps the stent her customer needed was available but hadn't yet been entered into inventory. It was a quest that sometimes yielded results, but not this time.

Then she contacted the sales team. Salespeople often had a small inventory of products with them for various reasons. But no one had the stent she needed.

Donna went to the company's inventory tracking system, and that's when she found it. There was the correct model stent in the correct size at a rival hospital in the same town as the one that needed it.

She called the rival hospital and got her contact there to agree to transfer the stent to the hospital that needed it. The stent arrived in time for the patient's procedure, thanks to Donna's extra effort.

Donna exhibited a uniquely human quality to solve the problem: advocacy. She actively worked on behalf of the hospital and its patient to create a better experience. While most customer service reps are content to follow the normal process and go no further, Donna kept going even when the normal process ran out.

In this chapter, we'll focus on the role humans play when things go wrong. We'll discuss the impact of *in*humane service, how automation can help or hinder a quest to find solutions, the importance of advocacy, and why customer service sometimes involves taking risks.

Why won't you help me?

Sandra Shuster knew her bag was in Chicago. United Airlines insisted it wasn't.

Shuster and her daughter, Ruby, had flown home to Denver from Baltimore, where Ruby had played in a lacrosse tournament. Ruby's lacrosse kit was too large to carry on, so they checked it.

Their flight connected through Chicago, but Ruby's lacrosse bag didn't make the connection. Shuster's Apple AirTag tracking device showed the bag was in United's Chicago baggage office. An airline representative at the lost luggage desk in Denver told Shuster the bag would come in on a later flight. It didn't.

Over the next six days, Shuster traded direct messages with United on Twitter. She made four calls to United's lost luggage phone line. Shuster even made three visits to the lost luggage desk in Denver, hoping a live person would be more helpful.

The solution seemed simple: contact Chicago and have a local employee retrieve the bag. Shuster's AirTag showed exactly where it was, but nobody would help. Employees didn't believe Ruby's bag was in

Chicago because the system said it wasn't. They were taught to trust the system, and strict policies prevented them from going around it.

United's baggage retrieval system relies on scanners to tell customer service agents where a bag is located. Employees are required to rely on the system because it's more efficient than manually contacting airport baggage offices and searching for lost bags one at a time.

The automated baggage tracking system works most of the time, but it's not infallible. The trouble with Ruby's lacrosse bag started in Baltimore when an airline employee accidentally put the wrong tag on it. That tag routed the bag to Chicago instead of all the way to Denver. That ensured the system would never flag Shuster's bag for forwarding to Denver without human intervention.

Some employees did believe Shuster when she explained the bag was stuck in Chicago, but they still wouldn't help. Employees told Shuster they weren't allowed to call the Chicago baggage office directly and there was nothing they could do. The employees worried about getting in trouble if they violated the policy.

Shuster finally took matters into her own hands. She took a day off work and booked a flight to Chicago using frequent flyer miles. It took the Chicago baggage claim office less than a minute to find Ruby's bag.[1]

A cascade of service failures caused this problem and prevented it from getting fixed. An employee error caused the system to fail. The system didn't have a way to recover. Transactional employees blindly followed a strict process designed to minimize human help. Employees were afraid of the repercussions for breaking procedure instead of being willing to do the right thing for a customer who needed them.

Just one person could have done the human thing and found a way to help. Somebody could have taken a risk and called Chicago. Or, if the Chicago number was protected from employees like Coca Cola guards its secret recipe, a humane employee could have found another way to advocate for the safe return of Ruby's bag. None of these things happened.

A lack of advocacy is at the heart of nearly every service failure. Something went wrong, and getting help was next to impossible. The solution was obvious, but an employee couldn't or wouldn't take action.

Transactional people use broken systems, rigid policies, and a lack of resources as excuses to stop trying. They don't advocate for their customer. They do what they're told and put in minimal effort.

You can almost sense an employee's relief when they've done all the procedure requires and flatly tell you, "Sorry, there's nothing I can do." They don't care whether or not you have a better experience. They don't view it as their job to make sure the mistake gets fixed, the promise gets kept, or the mess gets cleaned up. That's ultimately your problem, not theirs.

You might believe that solving problems is difficult in your company. The systems are set against you. You lack the resources, best practices, or authority to help. Maybe you've tried to help in the past and gotten nowhere or have even gotten in trouble.

I won't pretend it's easy. You might need to take risks or bend a few rules. It requires imagination, determination, and a willingness to do more than is strictly required.

Helping customers solve complex problems often means getting people on other teams to join in. Those coworkers might be reluctant to cooperate. Perhaps they're also worried about the danger of going around normal procedures.

Push too hard or go against the system and there could be consequences. You might get in trouble, fall short on productivity metrics, or develop a reputation for not being a team player. Employees in these environments quickly learn it's safer to do nothing instead of advocating on their customers' behalf.

I was one of those employees once. The company I worked for was thick with rules and bureaucracy. They were designed for efficiency and consistency, but they didn't always make sense. Sometimes the rigid rules caused delays and errors.

A customer called me with a very reasonable request to get an order shipped by a certain date. I instinctively told him it couldn't be done. But the only reason it couldn't happen was the corporate nonsense standing in the way.

I'll never forget what the customer said to me. "Isn't that what they're paying you for?"

He was right. I wasn't adding any human value if all I did was tell him why we couldn't deliver on time. I was acting like an automaton, telling the customer "no" without really trying. Worst of all, my company risked losing this customer's business if I couldn't respond.

His words struck a chord. I was determined to add human value and find a way to get his order shipped. It required extra effort and hustle. I had to navigate through a corporate bureaucracy that wasn't designed to accommodate reasonable customer requests. But I got it done.

The experience was enlightening. My quest to get that order out caused me to talk to people in other departments. I built cross-functional relationships and learned how to make their jobs easier so orders got through faster. The knowledge I gained helped me get future orders through more efficiently.

That company struggled with quality and efficiency. Finding a way around the system only works when you do it once in a while. It's not sustainable when you have to go the extra mile to solve every problem.

That's where AI can help.

AI helps but doesn't advocate

Amazon delivers orders with amazing accuracy.

There's a stunning amount of automation behind every order. Much of it is guided by AI making a flurry of logistical calculations and decisions.

Amazon's software scans available inventory and decides on the optimal warehouse from which to ship your order. For orders with multiple items, the system decides whether it's more efficient to ship everything together, or send multiple packages. Some orders require items to be pulled from multiple warehouses, and the software makes that decision, too.

The inside of an Amazon warehouse is a complex array of racks, conveyer belts, and other machines. Automation guides the way items are picked off shelves, routed to shipping stations, and expertly packed. It performs quality checks along the way to verify that orders are being processed correctly.

One tool Amazon uses to ensure your order contains the correct items is called the SLAM machine. SLAM stands for Scan, Label, Apply, and Manifest.

The SLAM machine weighs packaged orders and compares them to the expected weight for the shipment. It applies a shipping label if the weights match. Then the package is routed to the correct truck for shipment. If the weight is off, the box is automatically pushed off the shipping line into a quality control station for inspection.

Human employees inspect the shipments that the SLAM machine kicks out. They use their problem-solving skills to get to the bottom of the discrepancy and solve the issue before a customer is impacted.

I had a chance to tour an Amazon warehouse and see the SLAM machine in action. On the day of my tour, something went wrong and the SLAM machine began kicking out an unusually high volume of orders. An employee noticed the issue and immediately shut down the shipping line so the problem could be solved.

The issue was quickly identified. A shipping label had gotten stuck on one of the machine's sensors, which caused it to malfunction. The label was removed and the machine tested to make sure the problem was solved. Once the fix was confirmed, the line was restarted and packages began moving again. It took just a few minutes.

Like all machines, the SLAM machine doesn't care whether your order arrives accurately or on time. It simply does the job it was designed to do: scan packages to make sure they conform to expected standards and apply a shipping label if they do. It's up to a human to do the extra work on customers' behalf when the SLAM machine detects an irregularity.

There are many ways that AI can be a helpful problem-solving tool. It works best when it has human oversight, including safeguards to detect and resolve errors. Problems can get magnified when AI is allowed to be fully autonomous.

Hertz, a rental car company, has experimented with AI-powered technology to scan returned vehicles for damage. Customers reported the system was incredibly nit-picky, automatically charging people for the smallest of dents and dings that could be reasonably attributed to normal wear and tear. Some customers have even been billed for damage that appears to be merely dirt.

The fees for damage detected by the AI system can be steep. One customer was charged $80 to repair a dent plus $115 in processing fees. Images of the alleged dent didn't show any visible damage to the vehicle, but Hertz insisted there was a dent.[2]

Using technology for these types of "gotcha" tactics is anti-customer. AI can be a powerful tool to detect potential issues, like the SLAM machine Amazon uses to flag possible shipping errors. But using AI as judge and jury to mete out damage assessments without any oversight feels inhumane.

Customers deserve more than uncaring automatons or imperfect machines when something goes wrong. They deserve to have a real human work fiercely on their behalf. Someone like Donna, who doggedly pursued the right life-saving heart stent and wouldn't take "out of stock" for an answer.

Helping customers solve problems

There's something magical about small towns.

My wife and I once owned a vacation rental cabin in Idyllwild, a small mountain village in Southern California. We got to know a lot of service providers on a first-name basis. The town was small enough that everyone seemed to know everyone.

One day, I got a call from the water utility. "Hi, it's Cindy," the caller said. "Our crew was out reading meters this morning and noticed your water was running. It looks like you have a leak near the main shut-off valve."

Nobody likes to hear about a water leak, but it was refreshing to get a call from a real person who was looking out for me. I was able to call my property manager and get the leak repaired quickly. Cindy's advocacy saved me from an unexpectedly large water bill and possible damage from the running water.

Small town departments can do things like make personal calls. Cindy ran the office at the water district serving my mountain cabin. Call the water department, and Cindy would probably answer the phone. Send an email, and Cindy would be the one to receive it and reply. We'd spoken before, so I knew who Cindy was when she called.

That kind of personal service is impossible in areas with larger populations. But that shouldn't be an excuse for building systems and processes that don't allow customers to get help when something goes wrong. Humans can still be there to solve problems.

T-Mobile has been J.D. Power's top-rated wireless carrier for 15 years. One reason for the company's success is its Team of Experts program that provides access to localized human service when customers need it.[3]

The Team of Experts approach organizes customer care employees by geographic region. Each team specializes in caring for customers in that region. They're familiar with details like weather, network status, and T-Mobile retail stores. Customers can do a lot of things to manage their account using self-service, but they have the option to contact a live human dedicated to their region if they need extra assistance. That human is there to advocate on their behalf.

Making expert human customer service reps readily available has paid off. The company cut customer churn by 39 percent when it implemented the program while also cutting credits and bill adjustments in half. Calls per account decreased 37 percent with the Team of Experts model, and the overall cost to serve declined 26 percent.[4]

The team approach resonates with employees as well. They enjoy being able to provide real human service to their customers. Support agent turnover decreased by 49 percent after the Team of Experts model was implemented.

T-Mobile's competitors have finally taken notice. In 2025, both AT&T and Verizon announced their own more human-centric service models. These companies figured out that having humans available to advocate for customers is good for business.

Advocacy can also help build your reputation when others falter. Not long after Susan Shuster had to fly to Chicago to retrieve her daughter's lacrosse bag, United Airlines lost another piece of valuable luggage.

Luke Barnett was traveling home to Greenville, South Carolina, with his son, Gray. The two had been in Lyon, France, where Gray had been competing in a bicycle race. Their story is nearly identical to what happened to Susan Shuster and her daughter Ruby.

Gray checked his bicycle. It didn't make it home. Luke Barnett had an Apple AirTag that was packed with the bicycle, allowing him to identify its whereabouts. The AirTag showed the bicycle was in Brussels, Belgium, where the Barnetts had caught a connecting flight on their way to Greenville. Just like in Shuster's case, United Airlines wouldn't retrieve the bag.[5]

This is where the story took a different turn. Barnett contacted the airport customer service team in Brussels to ask them to intervene. A customer care agent named Ella was able to find the bicycle and get United Airlines to put it on a plane back to Greenville.

Finding and returning lost luggage is the airline's responsibility, not the airport's. It wasn't Ella's job to go searching for the bicycle or to get the airline to do its job. But she did. The bicycle might never have been returned if it wasn't for her advocacy and problem-solving skills. Human service succeeded where United's strict rules-based system failed.

Humans make the difference when something goes unexpectedly wrong. As a human, you can find ways around broken systems and rigid rules. You know the ins and outs of your company, so you can get things done that would be impossible without your help. AI can't.

Brian, my service advisor at Dalton Subaru, is an example of one of those people who works to make the customer experience better. He's one of the reasons why I stopped going to another mechanic that's closer to my home and instead take my car to get serviced at his dealership. I can count on Brian to advocate on my behalf when I need extra help.

A mechanic noticed a leak on a suspension strut as part of a routine maintenance visit. This was unexpected, because the strut needed to be replaced much sooner than the car's mileage would have predicted. And it was unfortunate because, despite having low mileage, the car was no longer under warranty.

Brian understood that unexpected costly repairs can break a customer's trust with an automotive brand and a dealership. He found a way to have the strut replaced at no cost to me as a goodwill gesture. Brian also made the repair convenient by arranging to have Lyft bring me home after dropping off my car and then bring me back to the dealership when the car was ready.

I know from experience that car dealerships don't always take care of customers in this way. Years ago, I had an Infiniti that I really loved. It was a G37 coupe with a manual transmission that was a ton of fun to drive. Unfortunately, I experienced a major transmission failure when the car had fewer than 40,000 miles. The warranty had expired, so it wasn't covered despite the low mileage. Neither Infiniti nor my local dealership would do anything to help with the costly repair. I still remember the unempathetic Infiniti customer care rep flatly refusing to even try to find a way to help me. I vowed never to buy another Infiniti.

Humans can't fix every problem, but when they act as advocates they can still help customers feel better. An insurance agent can't control skyrocketing insurance costs, but they can review a client's policy to make sure they're getting the best deal for the coverage they need. An appliance repair technician can't fix an old, broken oven that no longer has replacement parts available, but they can give their customer expert advice on what to look for in a new oven. Sometimes, just trying makes a difference.

The partner technique

One way to help customers solve problems is by using the partner technique.

The partner technique works as the name implies by positioning yourself as the customer's partner. In some cases, you literally stand on their side to help them solve an issue, as described in Chapter Five. At other times, such as serving a customer over the phone, it helps to imagine yourself standing beside them. The goal is to show the customer that you're on their team and want them to succeed.

I first discovered this technique while working with an airline client. One of the challenges for airline gate agents is monitoring over-sized carry-on bags as passengers board the plane. You're probably familiar with the baggage sizer next to the gate that your bag must fit in to be allowed on board.

Passengers often argued when my client's gate agents used a confrontational approach. The agent would face the customer with the bag and baggage sizer between them, creating a physical barrier that naturally prevented rapport. Agents used confrontational language: "Your bag has to fit in the baggage sizer or you'll have to check it." That might be the policy, but anxious passengers don't like being given commands as they're trying to board the plane.

Gate agents who used the partner technique got much better results. They stood next to the passenger so they could face the baggage sizer together. Those agents used partnership language like, "Let's measure your bag to see if it fits in the overhead bin." If the bag was too large, the agent quickly offered helpful options such as checking the bag at no cost or giving the passenger extra time to consolidate their luggage without losing their place in the boarding queue.

The partner technique means putting yourself on your customer's side and finding a way to help them have a better experience. Donna used it when she helped the hospital track down the right heart stent for a patient who desperately needed it. Ella used it to find Gray Barnett's bicycle and make sure United Airlines returned it. Brian used it to help me avoid a costly repair charge when my suspension strut met a premature demise.

Try using the partner technique with your customers. Stand next to them, or imagine yourself being literally on their side. Reassure your customer that you're there to help. Use your human instincts to find a way to solve the problem.

Solutions often present themselves when you choose to try, just like the enterprising person in the parking garage who figured out how to help the confused driver exit the garage (Chapter Six). Or Cindy in the water department who looked up my phone number so she could call and tell me my cabin had a water leak.

Those actions weren't in a manual somewhere. People figured out how to help by leaning into their humanity.

No technique works 100 percent of the time. There will be some customer problems you just can't solve. But you can still treat those customers with care. Many will appreciate knowing that you tried.

Let's recap

Humans can help customers solve problems that normal processes and automation can't fix. You sometimes have to bend a policy a bit or find an alternate route to give a customer the assistance they need and deserve.

The partner technique is one way to practice applying human service to problem-solving. It works by doing two things:

1. Putting yourself on your customer's side (literally, if possible).
2. Showing your customer you're there to find a solution.

You won't be able to fix every problem for every customer, but there are often more solutions available than you realize. Simply making the effort to help can make a customer feel better about their experience.

In our final chapter, we'll explore ways that you can partner with AI to unlock your super-human skills.

CHAPTER 7 NOTES

1   Julia Buckley, "The airline said her bag was lost, but her tracker said otherwise. So she flew to get it," (*CNN*, August 30, 2023), https://www.cnn.com/travel/article/airtag-lost-luggage-flight.

2   Gabe Castro-Root, "A.I. Is Making Sure You Pay for That Ding on Your Rental Car," (*The New York Times*, July 9, 2025), https://www.nytimes.com/2025/07/09/travel/rental-car-ai-scanner-hertz.html.

3   "Wireless Product Complexities and Evolving Customer Expectations Lead to Drop in Customer Care Satisfaction, J.D. Power Finds," J.D. Power press release, January 30, 2025, https://www.jdpower.com/business/press-releases/2025-us-wireless-customer-care-study-volume-1.

4   Callie Field, "How T-Mobile's Team of Experts Reinvented Customer Support," T-Mobile article, November 12, 2019, accessed January 11, 2026, https://www.t-mobile.com/business/resources/articles/reinventing-customer-service-with-team-of-experts.

5   Julia Buckley, "The airline lost his bike. He tracked it across the Atlantic," (*CNN*, September 5, 2023), https://www.cnn.com/travel/article/brussels-airport-lost-bike-airtag.

BONUS SECTION:
Super-Skills

The Human–AI Partnership

PRODUCT KNOWLEDGE TRAINING WAS TEDIOUS WORK IN 1998.

I was hired that year to supervise the contact center training department for a retailer that sold clothing via a printed catalog. One of my teams was responsible for educating our customer service agents on our products so they could quickly and accurately answer customer questions.

Our contact center's computer system was a precursor to the knowledge bases widely used today. Customer service agents could pull up images of catalog pages on their computer screen. They could click on product images to reveal an information box displaying product attributes, such as the fabric and care instructions. My team did a lot of manual work to create these clickable catalog pages and information boxes.

The team built each catalog page in the computer system, one at time. It was a painstaking process. First, they scanned in the physical catalog page. Next, the team hyperlinked each item on the catalog page by manually outlining the item on their screen. The hyperlink was set to trigger a pop-up text box with useful information about the product. The team had to type in that useful information so reps could access it while on the phone with a customer. The process had to be repeated for each item on each page in the catalog, and for every page in every new catalog version.

The team also staffed an internal product help hotline. Customer service reps could put a customer on hold and call the hotline if they encountered questions they couldn't answer. This was often more detailed information that didn't fit into those little hyperlinked text boxes.

The team had seven full-time employees to do all this work. It was a large investment, but giving customers accurate product information was vital. It gave people the confidence to order clothing via a catalog without being able to touch and feel it, as they would in a store. Sharing helpful information also helped prevent returns if a product was different from what the customer expected.

The system wasn't perfect. Agents had to know which catalog their customer had so they could pull up the correct page. It wasn't searchable by item number or product type, so agents had to identify the page their customer was viewing and manually pull it up on their screen. Those little text boxes had space for just a few lines of text, leaving room for only a few of the most commonly useful facts.

Agents still had to memorize basic product information since there was no place in the system to store general definitions or product types. For example, they had to know the difference between a scoop-neck and a boat-neck blouse so they could explain it to a customer who might care about those details.

Calling the product helpline required the agent to put the customer on hold. Our product helpline was typically staffed with just one person at a time, so the agent might have to wait to get connected. Once connected, it could take the product team member a few minutes to manually look up the answer. This put extra pressure on agents whose job performance was evaluated in part by how quickly they could get through calls.

We've come a long way since then. AI enables companies to provide employees with product knowledge resources quickly and automatically. It can pull data from multiple sources and instantly present it in an easy-to-read format.

One client implemented an AI-powered chatbot to answer product questions. The chatbot mined a deep repository of information on the company's website to quickly answer questions about any product they sell, so customers could use the chatbot for self-service product inquiries. Customer service reps used the same chatbot to answer questions when they were on the phone with a customer.

There are a number of advantages to this. Using the same source of knowledge that customers use ensures reps are giving the same answers customers would get if they looked up the information themselves. Reps also serve as quality control for the chatbot, since they're able to check its effectiveness and accuracy as they use it.

This is just one example of how AI is influencing customer service by replacing mind-numbing work that once required manual labor to complete, thereby freeing up customer service employees to spend more time providing human service.

In this chapter, we'll look at some of the ways AI can bring out your human service super-skills. This first example shows how it gives you the bandwidth to be human.

Bandwidth

AI can give humans more capacity by handling high-volume, repetitive tasks.

Fertitta Entertainment operates the Golden Nugget Hotel and Casino, which receives 100,000 phone calls per month. Most of those calls are routine, such as a guest who wants to redeem casino rewards points for a free hotel stay. An AI agent handles many of these calls, though guests have the option to transfer to a human if they prefer a more personal touch.

Brian Jeppesen is the Director of Contact Center Operations for Fertitta Entertainment. Jeppesen told me that the AI agent solved a huge customer experience problem. In 2021, up to 50 percent of customer calls were abandoned because the company couldn't hire enough employees to handle them all. Customers would call, get frustrated by the long wait time, and hang up.

The AI voice agent handled 87 percent of the call volume on the first day it went live. Guests got immediate assistance with basic requests, freeing agents to handle more complex inquiries or serve guests who were adamant about speaking to a human. The estimated return on investment from using AI to handle routine, transactional voice calls was a whopping 390 percent.

AI is best suited to handle customer-facing contacts that meet three criteria.

First, customers must be confident using AI to complete the task. Making a dinner reservation fits this criterion for most customers, though adding special requests for an anniversary dinner might be better suited for human service.

Second is that the task must be routine. Just like human employees, AI needs to be trained before it serves your customers. It needs to know the policies and procedures it must follow. Booking a hotel reservation is generally a routine transaction that's fairly straightforward for a properly-trained AI system. Helping a guest use a combination of cash and rewards points to book three rooms with specific features for a family trip probably calls for human expertise.

The third criterion is that results must be predictable. Customers should get the same answer to a question every time. For example, "What time do you close on Saturday?" should always yield the same correct answer. A more nuanced question like "Why did you close early last Saturday?" is better answered by a human who can be alert to a possible complaint.

Together, these criteria spell out the acronym CRaP: Confident, Routine, and Predictable. In other words, AI is great for the repetitive CRaP that burdens your employees with tedious work, is difficult to staff for, and creates unnecessary friction for customers when they're forced to wait for service. You'll likely find that customers are generally happy when CRaP gets automated since it makes it easier for them to complete simple tasks like making a reservation, checking a balance, or updating a password.

When AI handles the CRaP, customer service employees have more time to spend with customers who really need them. They can connect with customers, understand complex needs, and advocate for better outcomes when they aren't constantly challenged by queues of anxious customers waiting for assistance.

A good customer-facing AI system should have two fail-safes to ensure a positive experience. One is the ability to identify issues it can't solve on its own so it can escalate those to a human. The system should also recognize when a customer requests a human agent and escalate those as well. Those two capabilities prevent customers from getting stuck in a frustrating AI doom-loop where they can't get the human help they need or want.

Fail-safes that prevent customer frustration are also a starting point for unlocking AI's ability to supercharge human service.

Human super-skills

Members who call Heritage Federal Credit Union start their journey by speaking with Heidi, Heritage's AI voice assistant.

Heidi, which was developed by a company called Glia, works in concert with human agents to give members a seamless experience. It's able to resolve 34 percent of interactions on its own without involving an agent. Heidi remains an important team player for the remaining calls that benefit from human service.[1]

A member calls in to get help with a large loan and is immediately transferred to a human representative skilled in handling loan inquiries. In the past, that member would need to go to a branch to apply for their loan. Adding Heidi to the team has given Heritage's human contact center agents the bandwidth to add new skills for phone support, such as helping members with loan applications. Loan applicants no longer have to travel to their local branch, which has resulted in a 250 percent increase in loan growth for the credit union.

Another member calls in to report possible fraud. Heidi recognizes the potential complexity of the issue and transfers the call to a human agent. Heidi provides the agent with important details it's already gathered from the member, so the member doesn't have to repeat themselves. During the call, Glia's AI system monitors the conversation so it can provide the agent with real-time coaching on the best way to resolve the issue.

A third member calls to get help making a mobile deposit. This member is frustrated because they've tried mobile deposits several times and haven't been successful. They don't feel confident being served by AI, so they ask to be transferred to a human agent. The agent taking the call sees an AI-generated recap of the member's previous calls asking for help with mobile deposits, so they immediately know this is a situation requiring extra care and attention.

Glia's AI-powered software continues helping agents once the calls are complete. It automatically generates an after-call summary so agents don't have to spend time manually typing a recap of the call. These notes provide important context for future interactions, such as the member who called several times seeking help with mobile deposits.

This AI-human partnership has increased efficiency for Heritage's contact center. Average handle time decreased 18 percent. Handle time is a measure of the total length of a call plus any post-call work, like writing summary notes. Reducing handle time, along with AI resolving many interactions on its own, has allowed Heritage to double the amount of member contacts it handles without adding staff.

Systems like Glia's help humans shine in a number of ways. Contact center agents are given important context about the customer's needs and history, so they don't have to frustrate the customer by asking them to repeat themselves. They get real-time coaching and guidance from AI tools working in the background, so they can be more effective with each customer they serve.

AI is also improving training for customer service teams. Giving employees access to real-time coaching helps them learn procedures faster. Sharing knowledge at the right time reduces the need for time-consuming and error-prone memorization.

There are now AI systems that offer realistic role-play scenarios. These systems allow employees to practice conversations, write emails, or chat with customers, so they build their skills before interacting with real customers. Building skills in a controlled environment is especially useful for more challenging situations, such as defusing upset customers, that require extra finesse to handle effectively.

AI systems now have the ability to monitor customer conversations in real time and make suggestions about what humans should say or do. These systems learn as they go, revising their coaching based on what works and what doesn't. Employees get feedback from AI systems immediately after an interaction, so they can use those insights to do even better with the next customer they serve.

Managers can use AI-powered insights to quickly identify trends, such as a particular issue that's generating a lot of calls or a particular skill that multiple team members are struggling to perfect. AI can suggest coaching or training to improve performance. It can also flag individual employees who would benefit from additional feedback or assistance.

One technical support leader used AI to analyze the conversations her technical support reps were having with customers. She learned that customers bristled when an agent told them they'd "have to send a technician to their home" to diagnose and repair an issue. Customers were much happier when technical support reps used more positive positioning to schedule a technician. For example, telling the customer, "I'd like to have one of our technicians come to your home to look at this so we can resolve it as quickly as possible."

Using positive language is something many customer service professionals know about. Having AI run the numbers and provide data proving it works makes the business case.

Exercise: Find your AI partner

AI can help you expand your bandwidth and supercharge your human skills. The challenge is finding the right use case where AI will be an effective partner.

It helps to think of AI as a tool. Like any tool, choosing the right one to do a job can make the job a lot easier.

Is there a part of your job that's tedious, repetitive, and process-driven? Use the same framework we discussed earlier in this chapter for finding use cases for customer-facing AI: CRaP.

- **Confident:** Is there an AI tool you're confident about using for this task?

- **Routine:** Are there established standards for AI to follow?

  and

- **Predictable:** Can the AI tool perform the task consistently?

It helps to start small and work bigger. For example, the insurance company Allstate experimented with using AI to draft emails to customers who had filed insurance claims. The AI-crafted emails were more empathetic, less accusatory, and used less confusing jargon than emails written by human claims agents. Eventually, agents began using AI to draft nearly all of the 50,000 messages Allstate sends to customers each day. Human agents still review the emails for accuracy before sending them out, but using AI to draft messages enables agents to send better messages more quickly.[2]

Let's recap

We've come to the end of the book, so let's summarize the whole thing.

Human service means using uniquely human qualities to serve others. These qualities include connection, understanding, and advocacy. Companies like National Car Rental, Chick-fil-A, and Trader Joe's lead their industries by strategically using human service to add extra value.

Connection means establishing a human connection with a customer. This includes making them feel welcome with a warm greeting and building genuine rapport. Connections help customers know, like, and trust you, which enhances their perception of the service you provide.

Understanding involves deciphering your customers' unique needs. This includes listening beyond what your customers initially request to discern their deeper intent. It also requires you to pick up on your customers' emotional state so you can serve with empathy, helping customers feel better at the end of their experience than they did at the beginning.

Advocacy is actively working on behalf of your customer. It involves proactively looking for opportunities to add human value. Advocacy requires you to help customers solve problems, even if that means finding your way through or around obstacles, like broken products or restrictive policies.

AI can enhance your ability to provide human service.

You can increase your bandwidth to serve customers by using AI for tedious, repetitive work. This includes customer-facing tasks like simple inquiries or transactions. It also includes back-end tasks, like summarizing after-call notes or providing real-time coaching on how to better assist customers.

Look for CRaP you can automate with AI:

- **Confident:** the customer is (or you are) confident using AI for the task.
- **Routine:** there are established standards for AI to follow.

and

- **Predictable:** AI is able to achieve consistent results.

Human service is more than just a set of principles to follow. It's a mindset. You're a human with unique skills and qualities. Your customers are human, too. Focus on treating your customers humanely, and you'll consistently deliver great experiences and find more enjoyment and meaning in your work.

CHAPTER 8 NOTES

1   "Heritage Federal Credit Union: Turning the Contact Center into a Growth Engine," Glia website, accessed January 11, 2026, https://www.glia.com/case-study/heritage-fcu.

2   Isabelle Bousquette, "Turns Out AI Is More Empathetic Than Allstate's Insurance Reps," (*The Wall Street Journal*, February 10, 2025), https://www.wsj.com/articles/turns-out-ai-is-more-empathetic-than-allstates-insurance-reps-cf5f7c98.